Strange Interlude

Strange Interlude

A Play *by*

Eugene O'Neill

Jonathan Cape
Thirty Bedford Square London

FIRST PUBLISHED 1928
REPRINTED 1929
REPRINTED 1931
REPRINTED 1933
REPRINTED 1936
REPRINTED 1942
REPRINTED 1952
REPRINTED 1958
REPRINTED 1964

PRINTED IN GREAT BRITAIN BY
BUTLER AND TANNER LTD., FROME AND LONDON
BOUND BY A. W. BAIN AND CO. LTD.

Characters

CHARLES MARSDEN
PROFESSOR HENRY LEEDS
NINA LEEDS, *his daughter*
EDMUND DARRELL
SAM EVANS
MRS. AMOS EVANS, *Sam's mother*
GORDON EVANS
MADELINE ARNOLD

Scenes

FIRST PART

ACT ONE: Library, the Leeds' home in a small university town of New England – an afternoon in late summer.

ACT TWO: The same. Fall of the following year. Night.

ACT THREE: Dining-room of the Evans' homestead in northern New York state – late spring of the next year. Morning.

ACT FOUR: The same as Acts One and Two. Fall of the same year. Evening.

ACT FIVE: Sitting-room of small house Evans has rented in a seashore suburb near New York. The following April. Morning.

SECOND PART

ACT SIX: The same. A little over a year later. Evening.

ACT SEVEN: Sitting-room of the Evans' apartment on Park Avenue. Nearly eleven years later. Early afternoon.

ACT EIGHT: Section of afterdeck of the Evans' cruiser anchored near the finish line at Poughkeepsie. Ten years later. Afternoon.

ACT NINE: A terrace on the Evans' estate on Long Island. Several months later. Late afternoon.

FIRST PART

ACT ONE

SCENE: *The library of Professor Leeds' home in a small univer-*
sity town in New England. This room is at the front part
of his house with windows opening on the strip of lawn be-
tween the house and the quiet residential street. It is a
small room with a low ceiling. The furniture has been
selected with a love for old New England pieces. The walls
are lined almost to the ceiling with glassed-in bookshelves.
These are packed with books, principally editions, many of
them old and rare, of the ancient classics in the original
Greek and Latin, of the later classics in French and German
and Italian, of all the English authors who wrote while
s *was still like an* **f** *and a few since then, the most modern*
probably being Thackeray. The atmosphere of the room is
that of a cosy, cultured retreat, sedulously built as a sanc-
tuary where, secure with the culture of the past at his back,
a fugitive from reality can view the present safely from a
distance, as a superior with condescending disdain, pity, and
even amusement.

There is a fair-sized table, a heavy arm-chair, a
rocker, and an old bench made comfortable with cushions.
The table, with the Professor's arm-chair at its left, is
arranged toward the left of the room, the rocker is at centre,
the bench at right.

There is one entrance, a door in the right wall, rear.

It is late afternoon of a day in August. Sunshine,
cooled and dimmed in the shade of trees, fills the room with
a soothing light.

The sound of a maid's voice – a middle-aged woman –
explaining familiarly but respectfully from the right, and
Marsden enters. He is a tall thin man of thirty-five,

meticulously well dressed in tweeds of distinctly English tailoring, his appearance that of an Anglicized New England gentleman. His face is too long for its width, his nose is high and narrow, his forehead broad, his mild blue eyes those of a dreamy self-analyst, his thin lips ironical and a bit sad. There is an indefinable feminine quality about him, but it is nothing apparent in either appearance or act. His manner is cool and poised. He speaks with a careful ease as one who listens to his own conversation. He has long fragile hands, and the stooping shoulders of a man weak muscularly, who has never liked athletics and has always been regarded as of delicate constitution. The main point about his personality is a quiet charm, a quality of appealing, inquisitive friendliness, always willing to listen, eager to sympathize, to like and to be liked.

MARSDEN

    (*Standing just inside the door, his tall, stooped figure leaning back against the books – nodding back at the maid and smiling kindly.*)

I'll wait in here, Mary.

    (*His eyes follow her for a second, then return to gaze around the room slowly with an appreciative relish for the familiar significance of the books. He smiles affectionately and his amused voice recites the words with a rhetorical resonance.*)

Sanctum Sanctorum!

    (*His voice takes on a monotonous musing quality, his eyes stare idly at his drifting thoughts.*)

How perfectly the Professor's unique haven! . . .

    (*He smiles.*)

Primly classical . . . when New Englander meets Greek! . . .

    (*Looking at the books now.*)

He hasn't added one book in years . . . how old was I
when I first came here? . . . six . . . with my father . . .
father . . . how dim his face has grown! . . . he wanted to
speak to me just before he died . . . the hospital . . . smell
of iodoform in the cool halls . . . hot summer . . . I bent
down . . . his voice had withdrawn so far away . . . I
couldn't understand him . . . what son can ever understand? . . . always too near, too soon, too distant, or too
late! . . .

> *(His face has become sad with a memory of the*
> *bewildered suffering of the adolescent boy he had*
> *been at the time of his father's death. Then he*
> *shakes his head, flinging off his thoughts, and*
> *makes himself walk about the room.)*

What memories on such a smiling afternoon! . . . this
pleasant old town after three months . . . I won't go to
Europe again . . . couldn't write a line there . . . how
answer the fierce question of all those dead and maimed?
. . . too big a job for me! . . .

> *(He sighs – then self-mockingly.)*

But back here . . . it is the interlude that gently questions . . . in this town dozing . . . decorous bodies moving
with circumspection through the afternoons . . . their
habits affectionately chronicled . . . an excuse for weaving
amusing words . . . my novels . . . not of cosmic importance, hardly . . .

> *(Then self-reassuringly.)*

but there is a public to cherish them, evidently . . . and I
can write! . . . more than one can say of these modern sex-
yahoos! . . . I must start work to-morrow . . . I'd like to
use the Professor in a novel some time . . . and his wife
. . . seems impossible she's been dead six years . . . so
aggressively his wife! . . . poor Professor! now it's Nina
who bosses him . . . but that's different . . . she has bossed
me, too, ever since she was a baby . . . she's a woman now
. . . known love and death . . . Gordon brought down in
flames . . . two days before the armistice . . . what
fiendish irony! . . . his wonderful athlete's body . . . her

lover . . charred bones in a cage of twisted steel . . . no
wonder she broke down . . . Mother said she's become
quite queer lately . . . Mother seemed jealous of my concern . . . why have I never fallen in love with Nina? . . .
could I? . . . that way . . . used to dance her on my knee
. . . sit her on my lap . . . even now she'd never think anything about it . . . but sometimes the scent of her hair and
skin . . . like a dreamy drug . . . dreamy! . . . there's the
rub! . . . all dreams with me! . . . my sex life among the
phantoms! . . .

> (*He grins torturedly.*)

Why? . . . oh, this digging in gets nowhere . . . to the
devil with sex! . . . our impotent pose of to-day to beat the
loud drum on fornication! . . . boasters . . . eunuchs parad-
ing with the phallus! . . . giving themselves away . . .
whom do they fool? . . . not even themselves! . . .

> (*His face suddenly full of an intense pain and dis-
> gust.*)

Ugh! . . . always that memory! . . . why can't I ever
forget? . . . as sickeningly clear as if it were yesterday . . .
prep school . . . Easter vacation . . . Fatty Boggs and Jack
Frazer . . . that house of cheap vice . . . one dollar! . . .
why did I go? . . . Jack, the dead game sport . . . how I
admired him! . . . afraid of his taunts . . . he pointed to
the Italian girl . . . "Take her!" . . . daring me . . . I
went . . . miserably frightened . . . what a pig she was!
. . . pretty vicious face under caked powder and rouge . . .
surly and contemptuous . . . lumpy body . . . short legs
and thick ankles . . . slums of Naples . . . "What you
gawkin' about? Git a move on, kid" . . . kid! . . . I *was*
only a kid! . . . sixteen . . . test of manhood . . . ashamed
to face Jack again unless . . . fool! . . . I might have lied to
him! . . . but I honestly thought that wench would feel
humiliated if I . . . oh, stupid kid! . . . back at the hotel I
waited till they were asleep . . . then sobbed . . . thinking
of Mother . . . feeling I had defiled her . . . and myself
. . . for ever! . . .

> (*Mocking bitterly.*)

"Nothing half so sweet in life as love's young dream," what? . . .

(*He gets to his feet impatiently.*)

Why does my mind always have to dwell on that? . . . **too** silly . . . no importance really . . . an incident such as any boy of my age . . .

(*He hears someone coming quickly from the right and turns expectantly. Professor Leeds enters, a pleased relieved expression fighting the flurried worry on his face. He is a small, slender man of fifty-five, his hair grey, the top of his head bald. His face, prepossessing in spite of its too-small, over-refined features, is that of a retiring, studious nature. He has intelligent eyes and a smile that can be ironical. Temperamentally timid, his defence is an assumption of his complacent, superior manner of the classroom toward the world at large. This defence is strengthened by a natural tendency toward a prim provincialism where practical present-day considerations are concerned (though he is most liberal – even radical – in his tolerant understanding of the manners and morals of Greece and Imperial Rome!) This classroom poise of his, however, he cannot quite carry off outside the classroom. There is an unconvincing quality about it that leaves his larger audience – and particularly the Professor himself – subtly embarrassed. As Marsden is one of his old students, whom, in addition, he has known from childhood, he is perfectly at ease with him.*)

MARSDEN

(*Holding out his hand – with unmistakable liking.*)

Here I am again, Professor!

PROFESSOR LEEDS

(Shaking his hand and patting him on the back – with genuine affection.)

So glad to see you, Charlie! A surprise, too! We didn't expect you back so soon!

(He sits in his chair on the left of the table while Marsden sits in the rocker.)

(Looking away from Marsden a moment, his face now full of selfish relief as he thinks.)

Fortunate, his coming back . . . always calming influence on Nina . . .

MARSDEN

And I never dreamed of returning so soon. But Europe, Professor, is the big casualty they were afraid to set down on the list.

PROFESSOR LEEDS

(His face clouding.)

Yes, I suppose you found everything completely changed since before the war.

(He thinks resentfully.)

The war . . . Gordon! . . .

MARSDEN

Europe has "gone west" –

(He smiles whimsically.)

to America, let's hope!

(Then frowningly.)

I couldn't stand it. There were millions sitting up with the corpse already, who had a family right to be there –

(Then matter-of-factly.)

I was wasting my time, too. I couldn't write a line.

(*Then gaily.*)

But where's Nina? I must see Nina!

PROFESSOR LEEDS

She'll be right in. She said she wanted to finish thinking something out – You'll find Nina changed, Charlie, greatly changed!

(*He sighs – thinking with a trace of guilty alarm.*)
The first thing she said at breakfast . . . "I dreamed of Gordon" . . . as if she wanted to taunt me! . . . how absurd! . . . her eyes positively glared! . . .
(*Suddenly blurting out resentfully.*)

She dreams about Gordon.

MARSDEN

(*Looking at him with amused surprise.*)

Well, I'd hardly call that a change, would you?

PROFESSOR LEEDS

(*Thinking, oblivious to this remark.*)
But I must constantly bear in mind that she's not herself . . . that she's a sick girl . . .

MARSDEN

(*Thinking.*)
The morning news of Gordon's death came . . . her face like grey putty . . . beauty gone . . . no face can afford intense grief . . . it's only later when sorrow . . .
(*With concern.*)

Just what do you mean by changed, Professor? Before I

17

left she seemed to be coming out of that horrible numbed calm.

PROFESSOR LEEDS

(*Slowly and carefully.*)

Yes, she has played a lot of golf and tennis this summer, motored around with her friends, and even danced a good deal. And she eats with a ravenous appetite.

(*Thinking frightenedly.*)
Breakfast . . . "dreamed of Gordon" . . . what a look of hate for me in her eyes! . . .

MARSDEN

But that sounds splendid! When I left she wouldn't see anyone or go anywhere.

(*Thinking pityingly.*)
Wandering from room to room . . . her thin body and pale lost face . . . gutted, love-abandoned eyes! . . .

PROFESSOR LEEDS

Well, now she's gone to the opposite extreme! Sees everyone – bores, fools – as if she'd lost all discrimination or wish to discriminate. And she talks interminably, Charlie – intentional nonsense, one would say! Refuses to be serious! Jeers at everything!

MARSDEN

(*Consolingly.*)

Oh, that's all undoubtedly part of the effort she's making to forget.

18

PROFESSOR LEEDS

(*Absent-mindedly.*)

Yes.

(*Arguing with himself.*)
Shall I tell him? . . . no . . . it might sound silly . .
but it's terrible to be so alone in this . . . if Nina's mother
had lived . . . my wife . . . dead! . . . and for a time I
actually felt released! . . . wife! . . . helpmate! . . . now I
need help! . . . no use! . . . she's gone! . . .

MARSDEN

(*Watching him – thinking with a condescending
affection.*)
Good little man . . . he looks worried . . . always fuss-
ing about something . . . he must get on Nina's nerves. . . .
(*Reassuringly.*)

No girl could forget Gordon in a hurry, especially after
the shock of his tragic death.

PROFESSOR LEEDS

(*Irritably.*)

I realize that.

(*Thinking resentfully.*)
Gordon . . . always Gordon with everyone! . . .

MARSDEN

By the way, I located the spot near Sedan where Gordon's
machine fell. Nina asked me to, you know.

PROFESSOR LEEDS

(*Irritated – expostulatingly.*)

For heaven's sake, don't remind her! Give her a chance

to forget if you want to see her well again. After all, Charlie, life must be lived and Nina can't live with a corpse for ever!

(*Trying to control his irritation and talk in an objective tone.*)

You see, I'm trying to see things through clearly and unsentimentally. If you'll remember, I was as broken up as anyone over Gordon's death. I'd become so reconciled to Nina's love for him – although, as you know, I was opposed at first, and for fair reasons, I think, for the boy, for all his good looks and prowess in sport and his courses, really came of common people and had no money of his own except as he made a career for himself.

MARSDEN

(*A trifle defensively.*)

I'm sure he would have had a brilliant career.

PROFESSOR LEEDS

(*Impatiently.*)

No doubt. Although you must acknowledge, Charlie, that college heroes rarely shine brilliantly in after life. Unfortunately, the tendency to spoil them in the university is a poor training –

MARSDEN

But Gordon was absolutely unspoiled, I should say.

PROFESSOR LEEDS

(*Heatedly.*)

20

Don't misunderstand me, Charlie! I'd be the first to acknowledge –

(*A bit pathetically.*)

It isn't Gordon, Charlie. It's his memory, his ghost, you might call it, haunting Nina, whose influence I have come to dread because of the terrible change in her attitude toward me.

(*His face twitches as if he were on the verge of tears – he thinks desperately.*)

I've got to tell him . . . he will see that I acted for the best . . . that I was justified. . . .

(*He hesitates – then blurts out.*)

It may sound incredible, but Nina has begun to act as if she hated me!

MARSDEN

(*Startled.*)

Oh, come now!

PROFESSOR LEEDS

(*Insistently.*)

Absolutely! I haven't wanted to admit it. I've refused to believe it, until it's become too appallingly obvious in her whole attitude toward me!

(*His voice trembles.*)

MARSDEN

(*Moved – expostulating.*)

Oh, now you're becoming morbid! Why, Nina has always idolized you! What possible reason – ?

PROFESSOR LEEDS

(*Quickly.*)

I can answer that, I think. She has a reason. But why **she** should blame me when she must know I acted for the best — You probably don't know, but just before he sailed for the front Gordon wanted their marriage to take place, and Nina consented. In fact, from the insinuations she lets drop now, she must have been most eager, but at the time — However, I felt it was ill-advised and I took Gordon aside and pointed out to him that such a precipitate marriage would be unfair to Nina, and scarcely honourable on his part.

MARSDEN

(*Staring at him wonderingly.*)

You said that to Gordon?

(*Thinking cynically.*)
A shrewd move! . . . Gordon's proud spot, fairness and honour! . . . but was it honourable of you? . .

PROFESSOR LEEDS

(*With a touch of asperity.*)

Yes, I said it, and I gave him my reason. There *was* the possibility he might be killed, in the flying service rather more than a possibility, which, needless to say, I did not point out, but which Gordon undoubtedly realized, poor boy! If he were killed, he would be leaving Nina a widow, perhaps with a baby, with no resources, since he was penniless, except what pension she might get from the Government; and all this while she was still at an age when a girl, especially one of Nina's charm and beauty, should have all of life before her. Decidedly, I told him, in justice to Nina, they must wait until he had come back and begun to establish his position in the world. That was the square thing. And Gordon was quick to agree with me!

MARSDEN

(*Thinking.*)
The square thing! . . . but we must all be crooks where happiness is concerned! . . . steal or starve! . . .
(*Then rather ironically.*)

And so Gordon told Nina he'd suddenly realized it wouldn't be fair to her. But I gather he didn't tell her it was your scruple originally?

PROFESSOR LEEDS

No, I asked him to keep what I said strictly confidential.

MARSDEN

(*Thinking ironically.*)
Trusted to his honour again! . . . old fox! . . . poor Gordon! . . .

But Nina suspects now that you – ?

PROFESSOR LEEDS

(*Startled.*)

Yes. That's exactly it. She knows in some queer way. And she acts toward me exactly as if she thought I had deliberately destroyed her happiness, that I had hoped for Gordon's death and been secretly overjoyed when the news came!

(*His voice is shaking with emotion.*)

And there you have it, Charlie – the whole absurd mess!

(*Thinking with a strident accusation.*)
And it's true, you contemptible . . . !
(*Then miserably defending himself.*)
No! . . I acted unselfishly . . . for her sake! . . .

MARSDEN

(*Wonderingly.*)

You don't mean to tell me she has accused you of all this?

PROFESSOR LEEDS

Oh, no, Charlie! Only by hints – looks – innuendos. She knows she has no real grounds, but in the present state of her mind the real and the unreal become confused –

MARSDEN

(*Thinking cynically.*)
As always in all minds . . . or how could men live? . .
(*Soothingly.*)

That's just what you ought to bear in your mind – the state of hers – and not get so worked up over what I should say is a combination of imagination on both your parts.

(*He gets to his feet as he hears voices from the right.*)

Buck up! This must be Nina coming.

(*The Professor gets to his feet, hastily composing his features into his bland, cultured expression.*)

STRANGE INTERLUDE

> (*Thinking self-mockingly, but a bit worried about himself.*)

My heart pounding! . . . seeing Nina again! . . . how sentimental . . . how she'd laugh if she knew! . . . and quite rightly . . . absurd for me to react as if I loved . . . that way . . . her dear old Charlie . . . ha! . . .

> (*He smiles with bitter self-mockery.*)

PROFESSOR LEEDS

> (*Thinking worriedly.*)

I hope she won't make a scene . . . she's seemed on the verge all day . . . thank God, Charlie's like one of the family . . . but what a life for me! . . . with the opening of the new term only a few weeks off! . . . I can't do it . . . I'll have to call in a nerve specialist . . . but the last one did her no good . . . his outrageous fee . . . he can take it to court . . . I absolutely refuse . . . but if he should bring suit? . . . what a scandal . . . no, I'll have to pay . . . somehow . . . borrow . . . he has me in a corner, the robber! . . .

NINA

> (*Enters and stands just inside the doorway looking directly at her father with defiant eyes, her face set in an expression of stubborn resolve. She is twenty, tall, with broad square shoulders, slim strong hips and long beautifully developed legs – a fine athletic girl of the swimmer, tennis player, golfer type. Her straw-blond hair, framing her sunburned face, is bobbed. Her face is striking, handsome rather than pretty, the bone structure prominent, the forehead high, the lips of her rather large mouth clearly modelled above the firm jaw. Her eyes are beautiful and bewildering, extraordinarily large and a deep greenish blue. Since Gordon's death they have a quality of continually shuddering before some terrible*)

25

enigma, of being wounded to their depths and made defiant and resentful by their pain. Her whole manner, the charged atmosphere she gives off, is totally at variance with her healthy outdoor physique. It is strained, nerve-racked, hectic, a terrible tension of will alone maintaining self-possession. She is dressed in smart sport clothes. Too preoccupied with her resolve to remember or see Marsden, she speaks directly to her father in a voice tensely cold and calm.)

I have made up my mind, Father.

PROFESSOR LEEDS

(Thinking distractedly.)
What does she mean? . . . oh, God help me! . . .
(Flustered – hastily.)

Don't you see Charlie, Nina?

MARSDEN

(Troubled – thinking.)
She has changed . . . what has happened? . . .
(He comes forward toward her – a bit embarrassed, but affectionately using his pet name for her.)

Hallo, Nina Cara Nina! Are you trying to cut me dead, young lady?

NINA

(Turning her eyes to Marsden, holding out her hand for him to shake, in her cool, preoccupied voice.)

Hallo, Charlie!

(Her eyes immediately return to her father.)

Listen, Father!

MARSDEN

(*Standing near her, concealing his chagrin.*)
That hurts! . . . I mean nothing! . . . but she's a sick
girl . . . I must make allowance . . .

PROFESSOR LEEDS

(*Thinking distractedly.*)
That look in her eyes! . . . hate! . . .
(*With a silly giggle.*)

Really, Nina, you're absolutely rude! What has Charlie
done?

NINA

(*In her cool tone.*)
Why, nothing. Nothing at all.
(*She goes to him with a detached, friendly manner.*)
Did I seem rude, Charlie? I didn't mean to be.
(*She kisses him with a cool, friendly smile.*)
Welcome home.
(*Thinking wearily.*)
What has Charlie done? . . . nothing . . . and never will
. . . Charlie sits beside the fierce river, immaculately timid,
cool and clothed, watching the burning, frozen naked
swimmers drown at last. . . .

MARSDEN

(*Thinking torturedly.*)
Cold lips . . . the kiss of contempt! . . . for dear old
Charlie! . . .
(*Forcing a good-natured laugh.*)

Rude? Not a bit!

> (*Banteringly.*)

As I've often reminded you, what can I expect when the
first word you ever spoke in this world was an insult to me.
"Dog" you said, looking right at me – at the age of one!

> (*He laughs. The Professor laughs nervously. Nina
> smiles perfunctorily.*)

NINA

> (*Thinking wearily.*)
> The fathers laugh at little daughter Nina . . . I must get
> away! . . . nice Charlie doggy . . . faithful . . . fetch and
> carry . . . bark softly in books at the deep night. . . .

PROFESSOR LEEDS

> (*Thinking.*)
> What is she thinking? . . . I can't stand living like
> this! . . .
> (*Giggle gone to a twitching grin.*)

You are a cool one, Nina! You'd think **you'd** just seen
Charlie yesterday!

NINA

> (*Slowly – coolly and reflectively.*)

Well, the war is over. Coming back safe from Europe isn't
such an unusual feat now, is it?

MARSDEN

> (*Thinking bitterly.*)
> A taunt . . . I didn't fight . . . physically unfit . . . not
> like Gordon . . . Gordon in flames . . . how she must

resent my living! . . . thinking of me, scribbling in Press Bureau . . . louder and louder lies . . . drown the guns and the screams . . . deafen the world with lies . . . hired choir of liars! . . .

(*Forcing a joking tone.*)

Little you know the deadly risks I ran, Nina! If you'd eaten some of the food they gave me on my renovated transport, you'd shower me with congratulations!

(*The Professor forces a snicker.*)

NINA

(*Coolly.*)

Well, you're here, and that's that.

(*Then suddenly expanding in a sweet, genuinely affectionate smile.*)

And I *am* glad, Charlie, always glad you're here! You know that.

MARSDEN

(*Delighted and embarrassed.*)

I hope so, Nina!

NINA

(*Turning on her father – determinedly.*)

I must finish what I started to say, Father. I've thought it all out and decided that I simply must get away from here at once – or go crazy! And I'm going on the nine-forty tonight.

(*She turns to Marsden with a quick smile.*)

29

You'll have to help me pack, Charlie!

(*Thinking with weary relief.*)
Now that's said . . . I'm going . . . never come back
. . . oh, how I loathe this room! . . .

MARSDEN

(*Thinking with alarm.*)
What's this? . . . going? . . . going to whom? . . .

PROFESSOR LEEDS

(*Thinking – terrified.*)
Going? . . . never come back to me? . . no! . . .
(*Desperately putting on his prim severe manner
toward an unruly pupil.*)

This is rather a sudden decision, isn't it? You haven't
mentioned before that you were considering – in fact, you've
led me to believe that you were quite contented here – that is,
of course I mean for the time being, and I really think –

MARSDEN

(*Looking at Nina – thinking with alarm.*)
Going away to whom? . . .
(*Then watching the Professor with a pitying shudder.*)
He's on the wrong tack with his professor's manner . . .
her eyes seeing cruelly through him . . . with what terrible
recognition! . . . God, never bless me with children! . . .

NINA

(*Thinking with weary scorn.*)
The Professor of Dead Languages is talking again . . . a
dead man lectures on the past of living . . . since I was born
I have been in his class, loving-attentive, pupil-daughter
Nina . . my ears numb with spiritless messages from the

dead . . . dead words droning on . . . listening because he
is my cultured father . . . a little more inclined to deafness
than the rest (let me be just) because he is my father . . .
father? . . . what is father? . .

PROFESSOR LEEDS

(*Thinking – terrified.*)

I must talk her out of it! . . . find the right words! . . .
oh, I know she won't hear me! . . . oh, wife, why did you
die, you would have talked to her, she would have listened
to you! . . .

(*Continuing in his professor's superior manner.*)

– and I really think, in justice to yourself above all, you ought
to consider this step with great care before you definitely
commit yourself. First and foremost, there is your health to
be taken into consideration. You've been very ill, Nina, how
perilously so perhaps you're not completely aware, but I
assure you, and Charlie can corroborate my statement, that six
months ago the doctors thought it might be years before –
and yet, by staying home and resting and finding healthy
outdoor recreation among your old friends, and keeping your
mind occupied with the routine of managing the household –

(*He forces a prim playful smile.*)

and managing me, I might add! – you have wonderfully improved, and I think it most ill-advised in the hottest part of
August, while you're really still a convalescent –

NINA

(*Thinking.*)

Talking! . . . his voice like a fatiguing dying tune droned
on a beggar's organ . . . his words arising from the tomb of
a soul in puffs of ashes . . .

(*Torturedly.*)

31

Ashes! . . . oh, Gordon, my dear one! . . . oh, lips on my lips, oh, strong arms around me, oh, spirit so brave and generous and gay! . . . ashes dissolving into mud! . . mud and ashes! . . . that's all! . . . gone! . . . gone for ever from me! . . .

PROFESSOR LEEDS

(*Thinking angrily.*)

Her eyes . . . I know that look . . . tender, loving . . . not for me . . . damn Gordon! . . . I'm glad he's dead! . . .
(*A touch of asperity in his voice.*)

And at a couple of hours' notice to leave everything in the air, as it were –

(*Then judicially.*)

No, Nina, frankly, I can't see it. You know I'd gladly consent to anything in the world to benefit you, but – surely, you can't have reflected!

NINA

(*Thinking torturedly.*)

Gordon darling, I must go away where I can think of you in silence! . . .
(*She turns on her father, her voice trembling with the effort to keep it in control – icily.*)

It's no use talking, Father. I *have* reflected and I am going!

PROFESSOR LEEDS

(*With asperity.*)

But I tell you it's quite impossible! I don't like to bring up the money consideration, but I couldn't possibly afford – And how will you support yourself, if I may ask? Two years in

the University, I am sorry to say, won't be much use to you
when applying for a job. And even if you had completely
recovered from your nervous breakdown, which it's obvious
to anyone you haven't, then I most decidedly think you
should finish out your science course and take your degree
before you attempt –

> (*Thinking desperately.*)
> No use! . . . she doesn't hear . . . thinking of Gordon
> . . . she'll defy me . . .

NINA

> (*Thinking desperately.*)
> I must keep calm . . . I mustn't let go or I'll tell
> him everything . . . and I mustn't tell him . . he's my
> father . . .
> (*With the same cold calculating finality.*)

I've already had six months' training for a nurse. I will
finish my training. There's a doctor I know at a sanatorium
for crippled soldiers – a friend of Gordon's. I wrote to him
and he answered that he'll gladly arrange it.

PROFESSOR LEEDS

> (*Thinking furiously.*)
> Gordon's friend . . . Gordon again! . . .
> (*Severely.*)

You seriously mean to tell me you, in your condition, want
to nurse in a soldiers' hospital! Absurd!

MARSDEN

> (*Thinking with indignant revulsion.*)
> Quite right, Professor! . . . her beauty . . . all those men
> . . . in their beds . . . it's too revolting! . . .
> (*With a persuasive quizzing tone.*)

Yes, I must say I can't see you as a peace-time Florence Nightingale, Nina!

NINA

(*Coolly, struggling to keep control, ignoring these remarks.*)

So you see, Father, I've thought of everything and there's not the slightest reason to worry about me. And I've been teaching Mary how to take care of you. So you won't need me at all. You can go along as if nothing had happened – and really, nothing will have happened that hasn't already happened.

PROFESSOR LEEDS

Why, even the manner in which you address me – the tone you take – proves conclusively that you're not yourself!

NINA

(*Her voice becoming a bit uncanny, her thoughts breaking through.*)

No, I'm not myself yet. That's just it. Not all myself. But I've been becoming myself. And I must finish!

PROFESSOR LEEDS

(*With angry significance – to Marsden.*)

You hear her, Charlie? She's a sick girl!

NINA

(*Slowly and strangely.*)

I'm not sick. I'm too well. But they are sick and I must

34

give my health to help them to live on, and to live on myself.

(*With a sudden intensity in her tone.*)

I must pay for my cowardly treachery to Gordon! You should understand this, Father, you who –

(*She swallows hard, catching her breath.*)
(*Thinking desperately.*)
I'm beginning to tell him! . . . I mustn't! . . . he's my father! . . .

PROFESSOR LEEDS

(*In a panic of guilty fear, but defiantly.*)

What do you mean? I am afraid you're not responsible for what you're saying.

NINA

(*Again with the strange intensity.*)

I must pay! It's my plain duty! Gordon is dead! What use is my life to me or anyone? But I must make it of use – by giving it!

(*Fiercely.*)

I must learn to give myself, do you hear – give and give until I can make that gift of myself for a man's happiness without scruple, without fear, without joy except in his joy! When I've accomplished this I'll have found myself, I'll know how to begin living my own life again!

(*Appealing to them with a desperate impatience.*)

Don't you see? In the name of the commonest decency and honour, I owe it to Gordon!

35

PROFESSOR LEEDS

(Sharply.)

No, I can't see – nor anyone else!

(Thinking savagely.)

I hope Gordon is in hell! . . .

MARSDEN

(Thinking.)

Give herself? . . . can she mean her body? . . . beautiful body . . . to cripples? . . . for Gordon's sake? . . . damn Gordon! . . .

(Coldly.)

What do you mean, you owe it to Gordon, Nina?

PROFESSOR LEEDS

(Bitterly.)

Yes, how ridiculous! It seems to me when you gave him your love, he got more than he could ever have hoped –

NINA

(With fierce self-contempt.)

I gave him? What did I give him? It's what I didn't give! That last night before he sailed – in his arms until my body ached – kisses until my lips were numb – knowing all that night – something in me knowing he would die, that he would never kiss me again – knowing this so surely yet with my cowardly brain lying, no, he'll come back and marry you, you'll be happy ever after and feel his children at your breasts looking up with eyes so much like his, possessing eyes so happy in possessing you!

(Then violently.)

But Gordon never possessed me! I'm still Gordon's silly virgin! And Gordon is muddy ashes! And I've lost my happiness for ever! All that last night I knew he wanted me. I knew it was only the honourable code-bound Gordon, who kept commanding from his brain, no, you mustn't, you must respect her, you must wait till you have a marriage licence!

(*She gives a mocking laugh.*)

PROFESSOR LEEDS

(*Shocked.*)

Nina! This is really going too far!

MARSDEN

(*With a superior sneer – repelledly.*)

Oh, come now, Nina! You've been reading books. Those don't sound like your thoughts.

NINA

(*Without looking at him, her eyes on her father's – intensely.*)

Gordon wanted me! I wanted Gordon! I should have made him take me! I knew he would die and I would have no children, that there would be no big Gordon or little Gordon left to me, that happiness was calling me, never to call again if I refused! And I did refuse! I didn't make him take me! I lost him for ever! And now I am lonely and not pregnant with anything at all, but – but loathing!

(*She hurls this last at her father – fiercely.*)

37

Why did I refuse? What was that cowardly something in me that cried, no, you mustn't, what would your father say?

PROFESSOR LEEDS

(*Thinking – furiously.*)
What an animal! . . . and my daughter! . . . she doesn't get it from me! . . . was her mother like that? . . .
(*Distractedly.*)

Nina! I really can't listen!

NINA

(*Savagely.*)

And that's exactly what my father did say! Wait, he told Gordon! Wait for Nina till the war's over, and you've got a good job and can afford a marriage licence!

PROFESSOR LEEDS

(*Crumbling pitifully.*)

Nina! I – !

MARSDEN

(*Flurriedly – going to him.*)

Don't take her seriously, Professor!

(*Thinking with nervous repulsion.*)
Nina has changed . . . all flesh now . . . lust . . . who would dream she was so sensual? . . . I wish I were out of this! . . . I wish I hadn't come here to-day! . . .

NINA

(*Coldly and deliberately.*)

Don't lie any more, Father! To-day I've made up my mind to face things. I know now why Gordon suddenly

38

dropped all idea of marriage before he left, how unfair to me he suddenly decided it would be! Unfair to me! Oh, that's humorous! To think I might have had happiness, Gordon, and now Gordon's child . . .

(*Then directly accusing him.*)

You told him it'd be unfair, you put him on his honour, didn't you?

PROFESSOR LEEDS

(*Collecting himself – woodenly.*)

Yes. I did it for your sake, Nina.

NINA

(*In the same voice as before.*)

It's too late for lies!

PROFESSOR LEEDS

(*Woodenly.*)

Let us say then that I *persuaded* myself it was for your sake. That may be true. You are young. You think one can live with truth. Very well. It is also true I was jealous of Gordon. I was alone and I wanted to keep your love. I hated him as one hates a thief one may not accuse nor punish. I did my best to prevent your marriage. I was glad when he died. There! Is that what you wish me to say?

NINA

Yes. Now I begin to forget I've hated you. You were braver than I, at least.

PROFESSOR LEEDS

I wanted to live comforted by your love until the end. In short, I am a man who happens to be your father.

> (*He hides his face in his hands and weeps softly.*)

Forgive that man!

MARSDEN

> (*Thinking timidly.*)
> In short, forgive us our possessing as we forgive those who possessed before us . . . Mother must be wondering what keeps me so long . . . it's time for tea . . . I must go home . . .

NINA

> (*Sadly.*)

Oh, I forgive you. But do you understand now that I must somehow find a way to give myself to Gordon still, that I must pay my debt and learn to forgive myself?

PROFESSOR LEEDS

Yes.

NINA

Mary will look after you.

PROFESSOR LEEDS

Mary will do very well, I'm sure.

MARSDEN

> (*Thinking.*)
> Nina has changed . . . this is no place for me . . . Mother is waiting tea. . . .
> > (*Then venturing on an uncertain tone of pleasantry.*)

Quite so, you two. But isn't this all nonsense? Nina will be back with us in a month, Professor, what with the depressing heat and humidity, and the more depressing halt and the lame!

PROFESSOR LEEDS

(*Sharply.*)

She must stay away until she gets well. This time I do speak for her sake.

NINA

I'll take the nine-forty.

(*Turning to Marsden – with a sudden girlishness.*)

Come on upstairs, Charlie, and help me pack!

(*She grabs him by the hand and starts to pull him away.*)

MARSDEN

(*Shrugging his shoulders – confusedly.*)

Well – I don't understand this!

NINA

(*With a strange smile.*)

But some day I'll read it all in one of your books, Charlie; and it'll be so simple and easy to understand that I won't be able to recognize it, Charlie, let alone understand it!

(*She laughs teasingly.*)

Dear old Charlie!

41

MARSDEN

(*Thinking in agony.*)
God damn in hell . . . dear old Charlie! . . .
(*Then with a genial grin.*)

I'll have to propose, Nina, if you continue to be my severest critic! I'm a stickler for these little literary conventions, you know!

NINA

All right. Propose while we pack!

(*She leads him off, right.*)

PROFESSOR LEEDS

(*Blows his nose, wipes his eyes, sighs, clears his throat, squares his shoulders, pulls his coas down in front, sets his tie straight, and starts to take a brisk turn about the room. His face is washed blandly clean of all emotion.*)

Three weeks now . . . new term . . . I shall have to be looking over my notes. . . .

(*He looks out of window, front.*)

Grass parched in the middle . . . Tom forgotten the sprinkler . . . careless . . . ah, there goes Mr. Davis of the bank . . . bank . . . my salary will go farther now . . . books I really need . . . all bosh two can live as cheaply as one . . . there are worse things than being a trained nurse . . . good background of discipline . . . she needs it . . . she may meet rich fellow there . . . mature . . . only students here for her . . . and their fathers never approve if they have anything. . . .

(*He sits down with a forced sigh of peace.*)

I am glad we had it out . . . his ghost will be gone now . . . no more Gordon, Gordon, Gordon, love and praise and tears, all for Gordon! . . . Mary will do very well by me

. . . I shall have more leisure and peace of mind . . . and Nina will come back home . . . when she is well again . . . the old Nina! . . . my little Nina! . . . she knows and she forgave me . . . she said so . . . said! . . . but could she really? . . . don't you imagine? . . . deep in her heart? . . . she still must hate? . . . oh, God! . . . I feel cold! . . . alone! . . . this home is abandoned! . . . the house is empty and full of death! . . there is a pain about my heart! . . .

(*He calls hoarsely, getting to his feet.*)

Nina!

NINA'S VOICE

(*Her voice, fresh and girlish, calls from upstairs.*)

Yes, Father. Do you want me?

PROFESSOR LEEDS

(*Struggling with himself – goes to door and calls with affectionate blandness.*)

No. Never mind. Just wanted to remind you to call for a taxi in good time.

NINA'S VOICE

I won't forget.

PROFESSOR LEEDS

(*Looks at his watch.*)

Five-thirty just . . . nine-forty, the train . . . then . . . Nina no more! . . . four hours more . . . she'll be packing . . . then good-bye . . . a kiss . . . nothing more ever to say to each other . . . and I'll die in here some day . . . alone . . . gasp, cry out for help . . . the president will speak at the funeral . . . Nina will be here again . . . Nina in black . . . too late! . . .

(*He calls hoarsely.*)

Nina!

> (*There is no answer.*)

In other room . . . doesn't hear . . . just as well . . .

> (*He turns to the bookcase and pulls out the first
> volume his hands come on and opens it at random
> and begins to read aloud sonorously like a child
> whistling to keep up his courage in the dark.*)

"Stetit unus in arcem
Erectus capitis victorque ad sidera mittit
Sidereos oculos propiusque adspectat Olympum
Inquiritque Iovem;" . . .

(*Curtain.*)

ACT TWO

SCENE: *The same as Scene One, Professor Leeds' study. It is about nine o'clock of a night in early fall, over a year later. The appearance of the room is unchanged except that all the shades, of the colour of pale flesh, are drawn down, giving the windows a suggestion of lifeless closed eyes and making the room seem more withdrawn from life than before. The reading lamp on the table is lit. Everything on the table, papers, pencils, pens, etc., is arranged in meticulous order.*

Marsden is seated on the chair at centre. He is dressed carefully in an English made suit of blue serge so dark as to seem black, which, combined with the gloomy brooding expression of his face, strongly suggests one in mourning. His tall, thin body sags wearily in the chair, his head is sunk forward, the chin almost touching his chest, his eyes stare sadly at nothing.

MARSDEN

> *(His thoughts at ebb, without emphasis, sluggish and melancholy.)*

Prophetic Professor! . . . I remember he once said . . . shortly after Nina went away . . . "someday, in here, . . . you'll find me" . . . did he foresee? . . . no . . . everything in life is so contemptuously accidental! . . . God's sneer at our self-importance! . . .

> *(Smiling grimly.)*

Poor Professor! he was horribly lonely . . . tried to hide it . . . always telling you how beneficial the training at the hospital would be for her . . . poor old chap! . . .

> *(His voice grows husky and uncertain – he controls it – straightens himself.)*

45

What time is it? . . .

(*He takes out his watch mechanically and looks at it.*)

Ten past nine. . . . Nina ought to be here. . . .

(*Then with sudden bitterness.*)

Will she feel any real grief over his death, I wonder? . . .
I doubt it! . . . but why am I so resentful? . . . the two
times I've visited the hospital she's been pleasant enough
. . . pleasantly evasive! . . . perhaps she thought her father
had sent me to spy on her . . . poor Professor! . . . at least
she answered his letters . . . he used to show them to me
. . . pathetically overjoyed . . . newsy, loveless scripts,
telling nothing whatever about herself . . . well, she won't
have to compose them any more . . . she never answered
mine . . . she might at least have acknowledged them. . . .
Mother thinks she's behaved quite inexcusably . . .

(*Then jealously.*)

I suppose every single damned inmate has fallen in love
with her! . . . her eyes seemed cynical . . . sick with men
. . . as though I'd looked into the eyes of a prostitute . . .
not that I ever have . . . except that once . . . the dollar
house . . . hers were like patent leather buttons in a saucer
of blue milk! . . .

(*Getting up with a movement of impatience.*)

The devil! . . . what beastly incidents our memories
insist on cherishing! . . . the ugly and disgusting . . . the
beautiful things we have to keep diaries to remember! . . .

(*He smiles with a wry amusement for a second – then
bitterly.*)

That last night Nina was here . . . she talked so brazenly
about giving herself . . . I wish I knew the truth of what
she's been doing in that house full of men . . . particularly
that self-important young ass of a doctor! . . . Gordon's
friend! . . .

(*He frowns at himself, determinedly puts an end to
his train of thought and comes and sits down
again in the chair – in sneering, conversational
tones as if he were this time actually addressing
another person.*)

Really, it's hardly a decent time, is it, for that kind of speculation . . . with her father lying dead upstairs? . . .

> (*A silence as if he had respectably squelched himself – then he pulls out his watch mechanically and stares at it. As he does so a noise of a car is heard approaching, stopping at the kerb beyond the garden. He jumps to his feet and goes towards the door – then hesitates confusedly.*)

No, let Mary go . . . I shouldn't know what to do . . . take her in my arms? . . . kiss her? . . . right now? . . . or wait until she? . . .

> (*A bell rings insistently from the back of the house. From the front voices are heard, first Nina's, then a man's. Marsden starts, his face suddenly angry and dejected.*)

Someone with her! . . . a man! . . . I thought she'd be alone! . .

> (*Mary is heard shuffling to the front door, which is opened. Immediately, as Mary sees Nina, she breaks down and there is the sound of her uncontrolled sobbing and choking, incoherent words drowning out Nina's voice, soothing her.*)

NINA

> (*As Mary's grief subsides a trifle, her voice is heard flat and toneless.*)

Isn't Mr. Marsden here, Mary?

> (*She calls.*)

Charlie!

MARSDEN

> (*Confused – huskily.*)

In here – I'm in the study, Nina.

> (*He moves uncertainly toward the door.*)

NINA

(Comes in and stands just inside the doorway. She is dressed in a nurse's uniform with cap, a raglan coat over it. She appears older than in the previous scene, her face is pale and much thinner, her cheek bones stand out, her mouth is taut in hard lines of a cynical scorn. Her eyes try to armour her wounded spirit with a defensive stare of disillusionment. Her training has also tended to coarsen her fibre a trifle, to make her insensitive to suffering, to give her the nurse's professionally callous attitude. In her fight to regain control of her nerves she has overstriven after the cool and efficient poise, but she is really in a more highly strung, disorganized state than ever, although she is now more capable of suppressing and concealing it. She remains strikingly handsome and her physical appeal is enhanced by her pallor and the mysterious suggestion about her of hidden experience. She stares at Marsden blankly and speaks in queer flat tones.)

Hallo, Charlie! He's dead, Mary says.

MARSDEN

(Nodding his head several times – stupidly.)

Yes.

NINA

(In same tones.)

It's too bad. I brought Doctor Darrell. I thought there might be a chance.

(She pauses and looks about the room.)
(Thinking confusedly.)

His books . . . his chair . . . he always sat there . . . there's his table . . . little Nina was never allowed to touch

48

anything . . . she used to sit on his lap . . . cuddle against him . . . dreaming into the dark beyond the windows . . . warm in his arms before the fireplace . . . dreams like sparks soaring up to die in the cold dark . . . warm in his love, safe-drifting into sleep . . . "Daddy's girl, aren't you?" . . .

> (*She looks around and then up and down.*)

His home . . . my home . . . he was my father . . . he's dead . . .

> (*She shakes her head.*)

Yes, I hear you, little Nina, but I don't understand one word of it. . . .

> (*She smiles with a cynical self-contempt.*)

I'm sorry, Father! . . . you see you've been dead for me a long time . . . when Gordon died, all men died . . . what did you feel for me then? . . . nothing . . . and now I feel nothing . . . it's too bad . . .

MARSDEN

> (*Thinking woundedly.*)

I hoped she would throw herself in my arms . . weeping . . . hide her face on my shoulder . . . "Oh, Charlie, you're all I've got left in the world . . ."

> (*Then angrily.*)

Why did she have to bring that Darrell with her?

NINA

> (*Flatly.*)

When I said good-bye that night I had a premonition I'd never see him again.

MARSDEN

> (*Glad of this opening for moral indignation.*)

You've never tried to see him, Nina!

> (*Then overcome by disgust with himself – contritely.*)

Forgive me! It was rotten of me to say that!

NINA

(*Shaking her head – flatly.*)

I didn't want him to see what he would have thought was me.

(*Ironically.*)

That's the other side of it you couldn't dissect into words from here, Charlie!

(*Then suddenly asking a necessary question in her nurse's cool, efficient tones.*)

Is he upstairs?

(*Marsden nods stupidly.*)

I'll take Ned up. I might as well.

(*She turns and walks out briskly.*)

MARSDEN

(*Staring after her – dully.*)

That isn't Nina. . . .

(*Indignantly.*)

They've killed her soul down there! . . .

(*Tears come to his eyes suddenly and he pulls out his handkerchief and wipes them, muttering huskily.*)

Poor old Professor! . . .

(*Then suddenly jeering at himself.*)

For God's sake, stop acting! . . . it isn't the Professor! . . . dear old Charlie is crying because she didn't weep on his shoulder . . . as he had hoped! . . .

(*He laughs harshly – then suddenly sees a man outside the doorway and stares – then calls sharply.*)

Who's that?

EVANS

(*His voice embarrassed and hesitating comes from the hall.*)

50

It's all right.

(*He appears in the doorway, grinning bashfully.*)

It's me – I, I mean – Miss Leeds told me to come in here.

(*He stretches out his hand awkwardly.*)

Guess you don't remember me, Mr. Marsden. Miss Leeds introduced us one day at the hospital. You were leaving just as I came in. Evans is my name.

MARSDEN

(*Who has been regarding him with waning resentment, forces a cordial smile and shakes hands.*)

Oh, yes. At first I couldn't place you.

EVANS

(*Awkwardly.*)

I sort of feel I'm butting in.

MARSDEN

(*Beginning to be taken by his likable boyish quality.*)

Not at all. Sit down.

(*He sits in the rocker at centre as Evans goes to the bench at right.*)

(*Evans sits uncomfortably hunched forward, twiddling his hat in his hands. He is above the medium height, very blond, with guileless, diffident blue eyes, his figure inclined to immature lumbering outlines. His face is fresh and red-cheeked, handsome in a boyish fashion. His manner is bashful with women or older men, coltishly playful with his friends. There is a lack of self-confidence, a lost and strayed appeal-*)

*ing air about him, yet with a hint of some un-
awakened obstinate force beneath his apparent
weakness. Although he is twenty-five and has
been out of college three years, he still wears the
latest in collegiate clothes, and as he looks
younger than he is, he is always mistaken for an
undergraduate, and likes to be. It keeps him
placed in life for himself.)*

MARSDEN

(Studying him keenly – amused.)
This is certainly no giant intellect . . . overgrown boy
. . . likable quality though . . .

EVANS

(Uneasy under Marsden's eyes.)
Giving me the once-over . . . seems like good egg . . .
Nina says he is . . . suppose I ought to say something about
his books, but I can't even remember a title of one . . .
(He suddenly blurts out.)

You've known Nina – Miss Leeds – ever since she was a
kid, haven't you?

MARSDEN

(A bit shortly.)

Yes. How long have you known her?

EVANS

Well – really only since she's been at the hospital, although
I met her once years ago at a Prom with Gordon Shaw.

MARSDEN

(*Indifferently.*)

Oh, you knew Gordon?

EVANS

(*Proudly.*)

Sure thing! I was in his class!

(*With admiration amounting to hero-worship.*)

He sure was a wonder, wasn't he?

MARSDEN

(*Cynically.*)

Gordon über alles and for ever! . . . I begin to appreciate
the Professor's viewpoint . . .

(*Casually.*)

A fine boy! Did you know him well?

EVANS

No. The crowd he went with were mostly fellows who
were good at sports – and I always was a dud.

(*Forcing a smile.*)

I was always one of the first to get bounced off the squad
in any sport.

(*Then with a flash of humble pride.*)

But I never quit trying, anyway!

MARSDEN

(*Consolingly.*)

Well, the sport hero usually doesn't star after college.

53

Gordon did!

(*Eagerly – with intense admiration.*)

In the war! He was an ace! And he always fought just as cleanly as he'd played football! Even the Huns respected him!

MARSDEN

(*Thinking cynically.*)
This Gordon worshipper must be the apple of Nina's eye! . . .
(*Casually.*)

Were you in the army?

EVANS

(*Shamefacedly.*)

Yes – infantry – but I never got to the front – never saw anything exciting.

(*Thinking glumly.*)
Won't tell him I tried for flying service . . . wanted to get in Gordon's outfit . . . couldn't make the physical exam. . . . never made anything I wanted . . . suppose I'll lose out with Nina, too . . .
(*Then rallying himself.*)
Hey, you! . . . what's the matter with you? . . . don't quit! . . .

MARSDEN

(*Who has been staring at him inquisitively.*)

How did you happen to come out here to-night?

EVANS

I was calling on Nina when your wire came. Ned thought
I better come along, too – might be of some use.

MARSDEN

(*Frowning.*)

You mean Doctor Darrell?

(*Evans nods.*)

Is he a close friend of yours?

EVANS

(*Hesitatingly.*)

Well, sort of. Roomed in the same dorm with me at college. He was a senior when I was a freshman. Used to help
me along in lots of ways. Took pity on me, I was so green.
Then about a year ago when I went to the hospital to visit
a fellow who'd been in my outfit I ran into him again.

(*Then with a grin.*)

But I wouldn't say Ned was close to anyone. He's a dyed-
in-the-wool doc. He's only close to whatever's the matter
with you!

(*He chuckles – then hastily.*)

But don't get me wrong about him. He's the best egg ever!
You know him, don't you?

MARSDEN

(*Stiffly.*)

Barely. Nina introduced us once.

(*Thinking bitterly.*)

He's upstairs alone with her . . . I hoped it would be I
who . . .

55

EVANS

Don't want him to get the wrong idea of Ned . . . Ned's my best friend . . . doing all he can to help me with Nina . . . he thinks she'll marry me in the end . . . God, if she only would! . . . I wouldn't expect her to love me at first . . . be happy only to take care of her . . . cook her breakfast . . . bring it up to her in bed . . . tuck the pillows behind her . . . comb her hair for her . . . I'd be happy just to kiss her hair! . . .

MARSDEN

(*Agitated – thinking suspiciously.*)
What are Darrell's relations with Nina? . . . close to what's the matter with her? . . . damned thoughts! . . . why should I care? . . . I'll ask this Evans . . . pump him while I have a chance . . .
(*With forced indifference.*)

Is your friend, the Doctor, "close" to Miss Leeds? She's had quite a lot the matter with her since her breakdown, if that's what interests him!

(*He smiles casually.*)

EVANS

(*Gives a start, awakening from his dream.*)

Oh – er – yes. He's always trying to bully her into taking better care of herself, but she only laughs at him.

(*Soberly.*)

It'd be much better if she'd take his advice.

MARSDEN

(*Suspiciously.*)

No doubt.

EVANS

(*Pronounces with boyish solemnity.*)

She isn't herself, Mr. Marsden. And I think nursing all those poor guys keeps the war before her when she ought to forget it. She ought to give up nursing and be nursed for a change, that's my idea.

MARSDEN

(*Struck by this – eagerly.*)

Exactly my opinion.

(*Thinking.*)

If she'd settle down here . . . I could come over every day . . . I'd nurse her . . . Mother home . . . Nina here . . . how I could work then! . . .

EVANS

(*Thinking.*)

He certainly seems all for me . . . so far! . . .

(*Then in a sudden flurry.*)

Shall I tell him? . . . he'll be like her guardian now . . .

I've got to know how he stands . . .

(*He starts with a solemn earnestness.*)

Mr. Marsden, I – there's something I ought to tell you, I think. You see, Nina's talked a lot about you. I know how much she thinks of you. And now her old man –

(*He hesitates in confusion.*)

I mean, her father's dead –

MARSDEN

(*In a sort of panic – thinking.*)

What's this? . . . proposal? . . . in form? . . . for her hand? . . . to me? . . . Father Charlie now. eh? . . . ha!

57

. . . God, what a fool! . . . does he imagine she'd ever love him? . . . but she might . . . not bad-looking . . . likable, innocent . . . something to mother . . .

EVANS

(*Blundering on regardless now.*)

I know it's hardly the proper time —

MARSDEN

(*Interrupting – dryly.*)

Perhaps I can anticipate. You want to tell me you're in love with Nina?

EVANS

Yes, sir, and I've asked her to marry me.

MARSDEN

What did she say?

EVANS

(*Sheepishly.*)

Nothing. She just smiled.

MARSDEN

(*With relief.*)

Ah

(*Then harshly.*)

Well, what could you expect? Surely you must know she still loves Gordon?

58

EVANS

(Manfully.)

Sure I know it – and I admire her for it! Most girls forget too easily. She ought to love Gordon for a long time yet. And I know I'm an awful wash-out compared to him – but I love her as much as he did, or anyone could! And I'll work my way up for her – I know I can! – so I can give her everything she wants. And I wouldn't ask for anything in return except the right to take care of her.

(Blurts out confusedly.)

I never think of her – that way – she's too beautiful and wonderful – not that I don't hope she'd come to love me in time –

MARSDEN

(Sharply.)

And just what do you expect me to do about all this?

EVANS

(Taken aback.)

Why – er – nothing, sir. I just thought you ought to know.

(Sheepishly he glances up at ceiling, then down at floor, twiddling his hat.)

MARSDEN

(Thinking – at first with a grudging appreciation and envy.)
He thinks he means that . . . pure love! . . . it's easy to talk . . . he doesn't know life . . but he might be good for

59

Nina . . . if she were married to this simpleton would she
be faithful? . . . and then I? . . . what a vile thought! . . .
I don't mean that! . . .

(*Then forcing a kindly tone.*)

You see, there's really nothing I can do about it.

(*With a smile.*)

If Nina will, she will – and if she won't, she won't. But I
can wish you good luck.

EVANS

(*Immediately all boyish gratitude.*)

Thanks! That's darn fine of you, Mr. Marsden!

MARSDEN

But I think we'd better let the subject drop, don't you?
We're forgetting that her father –

EVANS

(*Guiltily embarrassed.*)

Yes – sure – I'm a damn fool! Excuse me!

(*There is the noise of steps from the hall and Doctor
Edmund Darrell enters. He is twenty-seven,
short, dark, wiry, his movements rapid and sure,
his manner cool and observant, his dark eyes
analytical. His head is handsome and intelligent. There is a quality about him, provoking
and disturbing to women, of intense passion
which he has rigidly trained himself to control
and set free only for the objective satisfaction of
studying his own and their reactions: and so he
has come to consider himself as immune to love*)

STRANGE INTERLUDE

*through his scientific understanding of its real
sexual nature. He sees Evans and Marsden,
nods at Marsden silently, who returns it coldly,
goes to the table and taking a prescription pad
from his pocket, hastily scratches on it.)*

MARSDEN

(Thinking sneeringly.)

Amusing, these young doctors! . . . perspire with the
effort to appear cool! . . . writing a prescription . . . cough
medicine for the corpse, perhaps! . . . good-looking? . . .
more or less . . . attractive to women, I dare say. . . .

DARRELL

(Tears it off – hands it to Evans.)

Here, Sam. Run along up the street and get this filled.

EVANS

(With relief.)

Sure. Glad of the chance for a walk.

(He goes out, rear.)

DARRELL

(Turning to Marsden.)

It's for Nina. She's got to get some sleep to-night.

*(He sits down abruptly in the chair at centre. Mars-
den unconsciously takes the Professor's place
behind the table. The two men stare at each
other for a moment, Darrell with a frank prob-
ing, examining look that ruffles Marsden and
makes him all the more resentful toward him.)*

This Marsden doesn't like me . . . that's evident . . .

61

but he interests me . . . read his books . . . wanted to know his bearing on Nina's case . . . his novels just well-written surface . . . no depth, no digging underneath . . . why? . . . has the talent but doesn't dare . . . afraid he'll meet himself somewhere . . . one of those poor devils who spend their lives trying not to discover which sex they belong to! . . .

MARSDEN

Giving me the fishy, diagnosing eye they practise at medical school . . . like freshmen from Ioway cultivating broad A's at Harvard! . . . what is his specialty? . . . neurologist, I think . . . I hope not psychoanalyst . . . a lot to account for, Herr Freud! . . . punishment to fit his crimes, be forced to listen eternally during breakfast while innumerable plain ones tell him dreams about snakes . . . pah, what an easy cure-all! . . . sex the philosopher's stone . . . "O Oedipus, O my king! The world is adopting you!" . . .

DARRELL

Must pitch into him about Nina . . . have to have his help . . . damn little time to convince him . . . he's the kind you have to explode a bomb under to get them to move . . . but not too big a bomb . . . they blow to pieces easily . . .

(*Brusquely*.)

Nina's gone to pot again! Not that her father's death is a shock in the usual sense of grief. I wish to God it were! No, it's a shock because it's finally convinced her she can't feel anything any more. That's what she's doing upstairs now — trying to goad herself into feeling something!

MARSDEN

(*Resentfully*.)

I think you're mistaken. She loved her father –

DARRELL

(*Shortly and dryly.*)

We can't waste time being sentimental, Marsden! She'll be down any minute, and I've got a lot to talk over with you.

(*As Marsden seems again about to protest.*)

Nina has a real affection for you and I imagine you have for her. Then you'll want as much as I do to get her straightened out. She's a corking girl. She ought to have every chance for a happy life.

(*Then sharply driving his words in.*)

But the way she's conditioned now, there's no chance. She's piled on too many destructive experiences. A few more and she'll dive for the gutter just to get the security that comes from knowing she's touched bottom and there's no farther to go!

MARSDEN

(*Revolted and angry, half springs to his feet.*)

Look here, Darrell, I'll be damned if I'll listen to such a ridiculous statement!

DARRELL

(*Curtly – with authority.*)

How do you know it's ridiculous? What do you know of Nina since she left home? But she hadn't been nursing with us three days before I saw she really ought to be a patient; and ever since then I've studied her case. So I think it's up to you to listen.

63

MARSDEN

(*Freezingly.*)

I'm listening.

(*With apprehensive terror.*)

Gutter . . . has she . . . I wish he wouldn't tell me! . . .

DARRELL

(*Thinking.*)

How much need I tell him? . . . can't tell him the raw truth about her promiscuity . . . he isn't built to face reality . . . no writer is outside of his books . . . have to tone it down for him . . . but not too much! . . .

Nina has been giving way more and more to a morbid longing for martyrdom. The reason for it is obvious. Gordon went away without – well, let's say marrying her. The war killed him. She was left suspended. Then she began to blame herself and to want to sacrifice herself and at the same time give happiness to various fellow war-victims by pretending to love them. It's a pretty idea, but it hasn't worked out. Nina's a bad actress. She hasn't convinced the men of her love – or herself of her good intentions. And each experience of this kind has only left her more a prey to a guilty conscience than before and more determined to punish herself!

MARSDEN

(*Thinking.*)

What does he mean? . . . how far did she? . . . how many? . . .

(*Coldly and sneeringly.*)

May I ask on what specific actions of hers this theory of yours is based?

DARRELL

On her evident craving to make an exhibition of kissing,
necking, petting – whatever you call it – spooning in general
– with any patient in the institution who got a case on her!

(*Ironically – thinking.*)
Spooning! . . . rather a mild word for her affairs . . .
but strong enough for this ladylike soul. . . .

MARSDEN

(*Bitterly.*)
He's lying! . . . what's he trying to hide? . . . was he one
of them? . . . her lover? . . . I must get her away from him
. . . get her to marry Evans! . . .
(*With authority.*)

Then she mustn't go back to your hospital, that's certain!

DARRELL

(*Quickly.*)
You're quite right. And that brings me to what I want
you to urge her to do.

MARSDEN

(*Thinking suspiciously.*)
He doesn't want her back . . . I must have been wrong
. . . but there might be many reasons why he'd wish to get
rid of her . . .
(*Coldly.*)

I think you exaggerate my influence.

DARRELL

(*Eagerly.*)
Not a bit. You're the last link connecting her with the girl
she used to be before Gordon's death. You're closely associ-

c

ated in her mind with that period of happy security, of health and peace of mind. I know that from the way she talks about you. You're the only person she still respects – and really loves.

> (*As Marsden starts guiltily and glances at him in confusion – with a laugh.*)

Oh, you needn't look frightened. I mean the sort of love she'd feel for an uncle.

MARSDEN

> (*Thinking in agony.*)
> Frightened? . . . was I? . . . only person she loves . . . and then he said "love she'd feel for an uncle" . . . Uncle Charlie now! . . . God damn him! . . .

DARRELL

> (*Eyeing him.*)
> Looks damnably upset . . . wants to evade all responsibility for her, I suppose . . . he's that kind . . . all the better! . . . he'll be only too anxious to get her safely married. . . .
> (*Bluntly.*)

And that's why I've done all this talking. You've got to help snap her out of this.

MARSDEN

> (*Bitterly.*)

And how, if I may ask?

DARRELL

There's only one way I can see. Get her to marry Sam Evans.

MARSDEN

(*Astonished.*)

Evans?

(*He makes a silly gesture toward the door.*)
(*Thinking confusedly.*)
Wrong again . . . why does he want her married to . . .
it's some trick. . . .

DARRELL

Yes, Evans. He's in love with her. And it's one of those
unselfish loves you read about. And she is fond of him. In a
maternal way, of course – but that's just what she needs now,
someone she cares about to mother and boss and keep her
occupied. And still more important, this would give her a
chance to have children. She's got to find normal outlets for
her craving for sacrifice. She needs normal love objects for
the emotional life Gordon's death blocked up in her. Now
marrying Sam ought to do the trick. Ought to. Naturally,
no one can say for certain. But I think his unselfish love,
combined with her real liking for him, will gradually give her
back a sense of security and a feeling of being worth something to life again, and once she's got that, she'll be saved!

(*He has spoken with persuasive feeling. He asks
anxiously.*)

Doesn't that seem good sense to you?

MARSDEN

(*Suspicious – dryly non-committal.*)

I'm sorry, but I'm in no position to say. I don't know anything about Evans, for one thing.

67

DARRELL

(*Emphatically.*)

Well, I do. He's a fine healthy boy, clean and unspoiled. You can take my word for that. And I'm convinced he's got the right stuff in him to succeed, once he grows up and buckles down to work. He's only a big kid now, but all he needs is a little self-confidence and a sense of responsibility. He's holding down a fair job, too, considering he's just started in the advertising game – enough to keep them living.

(*With a slight smile.*)

I'm prescribing for Sam, too, when I boost this wedding.

MARSDEN

(*His snobbery coming out.*)

Do you know his family – what sort of people? –

DARRELL

(*Bitingly.*)

I'm not acquainted with their social qualifications, if that's what you mean! They're up-state country folks – fruit growers and farmers, well off, I believe. Simple, healthy people, I'm sure of that although I've never met them.

MARSDEN

(*A bit shamefacedly – changing the subject hastily.*)

Have you suggested this match to Nina?

DARRELL

Yes, a good many times lately in a half-joking way. If I were serious she wouldn't listen, she'd say I was prescribing.

But I think what I've said has planted it in her mind as a possibility.

MARSDEN

(*Thinking suspiciously.*)
Is this Doctor her lover? . . . trying to pull the wool over my eyes? . . . use me to arrange a convenient triangle for him? . . .
(*Harshly – but trying to force a joking tone.*)

Do you know what I'm inclined to suspect, Doctor? That you may be in love with Nina yourself!

DARRELL

(*Astonished.*)

The deuce you do! What the devil makes you think that? Not that any man mightn't fall in love with Nina. Most of them do. But I didn't happen to. And what's more I never could. In my mind she always belongs to Gordon. It's probably a reflection of her own silly fixed idea about him.

(*Suddenly, dryly and harshly.*)

And I couldn't share a woman – even with a ghost!

(*Thinking cynically.*)
Not to mention the living who have had her! . . . Sam doesn't know about them . . . and I'll bet he couldn't believe it of her even if she confessed! . . .

MARSDEN

(*Thinking baffledly.*)
Wrong again! . . . he isn't lying . . . but I feel he's hiding something . . . why does he speak so resentfully of Gordon's memory? . . . why do I sympathize? . . .
(*In a strange mocking ironic tone.*)

I can quite appreciate your feeling about Gordon. I wouldn't care to share with a ghost-lover myself. That species of dead is so invulnerably alive! Even a doctor couldn't kill one, eh?

> (*He forces a laugh – then in a friendly confidential tone.*)

Gordon is too egregious for a ghost. That was the way Nina's father felt about him, too.

> (*Suddenly reminded of the dead man – in penitently sad tones.*)

You didn't know her father, did you? A charming old fellow!

DARRELL

> (*Hearing a noise from the hall – warningly.*)

Sstt!

> (*Nina enters slowly. She looks from one to the other with a queer, quick, inquisitive stare, but her face is a pale expressionless mask drained of all emotional response to human contacts. It is as if her eyes were acting on their own account as restless, prying, recording instruments. The two men have risen and stare at her anxiously. Darrell moves back and to one side until he is standing in relatively the same place as Marsden had occupied in the previous scene, while Marsden is in her father's place, and she stops where she had been. There is a pause. Then just as each of the men is about to speak, she answers as if they had asked a question.*)

NINA

> (*In a queer flat voice.*)

Yes, he's dead – my father – whose passion created me – who began me – he is ended. There is only his end living –

70

his death. It lives now to draw nearer me, to draw me nearer, to become my end!

(Then with a strange twisted smile.)

How we poor monkeys hide from ourselves behind the sounds called words!

MARSDEN

(Thinking frightenedly.)
How terrible she is! . . . who is she? . . . not my Nina! . . .
(As if to reassure himself – timidly.)
Nina!

(Darrell makes an impatient gesture for him to let her go on. What she is saying interests him and he feels talking it out will do her good. She looks at Marsden for a moment startledly as if she couldn't recognize him.)

NINA

What?

(Then placing him – with real affection that is like a galling goad to him.)
Dear old Charlie!

MARSDEN

Dear damned Charlie! . . . She loves to torture! . . .
(Then forcing a smile – soothingly.)
Yes, Nina Cara Nina! Right here!

NINA

(Forcing a smile.)

You look frightened, Charlie. Do I seem queer? It's because I've suddenly seen the lies in the sounds called words.

71

You know – grief, sorrow, love, father – those sounds our lips make and our hands write. You ought to know what I mean. You work with them. Have you written another novel lately? But, stop to think, you're just the one who couldn't know what I mean. With you the lies have become the only truthful things. And I suppose that's the logical conclusion to the whole evasive mess, isn't it? Do you understand me, Charlie? Say lie –

(*She says it, drawing it out.*)

L-i-i-e! Now say life. L-i-i-f-e! You see! Life is just a long drawn out lie with a sniffling sigh at the end!

(*She laughs.*)

MARSDEN

(*In strange agony.*)

She's hard! . . . like a whore! . . . tearing your heart with dirty finger nails! . . . my Nina! . . . cruel bitch! . . . some day I won't bear it! . . . I'll scream out the truth about every woman! . . . no kinder at heart than dollar tarts! . . .

(*Then in a passion of remorse.*)

Forgive me, Mother! . . . I didn't mean all! . .

DARRELL

(*A bit worried himself now – persuasively.*)

Why not sit down, Nina, and let us two gentlemen sit down?

NINA

(*Smiling at him swiftly and mechanically.*)

Oh, all right, Ned.

(*She sits at centre. He comes and sits on the bench. Marsden sits by the table. She continues sarcastically.*)

72

Are you prescribing for me again, Ned? This is my pet doctor, Charlie. He couldn't be happy in heaven unless God called him in because He'd caught something! Did you ever know a young scientist, Charlie? He believes if you pick a lie to pieces, the pieces are the truth! I like him because he's so inhuman. But once he kissed me – in a moment of carnal weakness! I was as startled as if a mummy had done it! And then he looked so disgusted with himself! I had to laugh!

(She smiles at him with a pitying scorn.)

DARRELL

(Good-naturedly smiling.)

That's right! Rub it in!

(Ruffled but amused in spite of it.)
I'd forgotten about that kiss . . . I was sore at myself afterwards . . . she was so damned indifferent! . . .

NINA

(Wanderingly.)

Do you know what I was doing upstairs? I was trying to pray. I tried hard to pray to the modern science God. I thought of a million light years to a spiral nebula – one other universe among innumerable others. But how could that God care about our trifling misery of death-born-of-birth? I couldn't believe in Him, and I wouldn't if I could! I'd rather imitate His indifference and prove I had that one trait at least in common!

MARSDEN

(Worriedly.)

Nina, why don't you lie down?

NINA

(*Jeeringly.*)

Oh, let me talk, Charlie! They're only words, remember! So many, many words have jammed up into thoughts in my poor head! You'd better let them overflow or they'll burst the dam! I wanted to believe in any God at any price – a heap of stones, a mud image, a drawing on a wall, a bird, a fish, a snake, a baboon – or even a good man preaching the simple platitudes of truth, those Gospel words we love the sound of but whose meaning we pass on to spooks to live by!

MARSDEN

(*Again – half rising – frightenedly.*)

Nina! You ought to stop talking. You'll work yourself into –

(*He glances angrily at Darrell as if demanding that, as a doctor, he do something.*)

NINA

(*With bitter hopelessness.*)

Oh, all right!

DARRELL

(*Answering his look – thinking.*)
You poor fool! . . . it'll do her good to talk this out of her system . . . and then it'll be up to you to bring her around to Sam . . .
(*Starts toward the door.*)

Think I'll go out and stretch my legs.

STRANGE INTERLUDE

MARSDEN

(*Thinking – in a panic.*)
I don't want to be alone with her! . . . I don't know her!
. . . I'm afraid! . . .
          (*Protestingly.*)

Well – but – hold on – I'm sure Nina would rather –

NINA

(*Dully.*)

Let him go. I've said everything I can ever say – to him.
I want to talk to you, Charlie.

          (*Darrell goes out noiselessly with a meaning look at
          Marsden – a pause.*)

MARSDEN

(*Thinking tremblingly.*)
Here . . . now . . . what I hoped . . . she and I alone
. . . she will cry . . . I will comfort her . . . why am I so
afraid? . . whom do I fear? . . . is it she? . . . or I? . . .

NINA

(*Suddenly, with pity yet with scorn.*)

Why have you always been so timid, Charlie? Why are
you always afraid? What are you afraid of?

MARSDEN

(*Thinking in a panic.*)
She sneaked into my soul to spy! . . .
          (*Then boldly.*)

Well, then, a little truth for once in a way! . . .
(Timidly.)

I'm afraid of – of life, Nina

NINA

(Nodding slowly.)

I know.

(After a pause – queerly.)

The mistake began when God was created in a male image. Of course, women would see Him that way, but men should have been gentlemen enough, remembering their mothers, to make God a woman! But the God of gods – the Boss – has always been a man. That makes life so perverted, and death so unnatural. We should have imagined life as created in the birth-pain of God the Mother. Then we would understand why we, Her children, have inherited pain, for we would know that our life's rhythm beats from Her great heart, torn with the agony of love and birth. And we would feel that death meant reunion with Her, a passing back into Her substance, blood of Her blood again, peace of Her peace!

(Marsden has been listening to her fascinatedly. She gives a strange little laugh.)

Now wouldn't that be more logical and satisfying than having God a male whose chest thunders with egotism and is too hard for tired heads and thoroughly comfortless? Wouldn't it, Charlie?

MARSDEN

(With a strange passionate eagerness.)

Yes! It would, indeed! It would, Nina!

NINA

(Suddenly jumping to her feet and going to him – with a horrible moaning desolation.)

Oh, God, Charlie, I want to believe in something! I want to believe so I can feel! I want to feel that he is dead – my father! And I can't feel anything, Charlie! I can't feel anything at all!

> *(She throws herself on her knees beside him and hides her face in her hands on his knees and begins to sob – stifled torn sounds.)*

MARSDEN

(Bends down, pats her head with trembling hands, soothes her with uncertain trembling words.)

There – there – don't – Nina, please – don't cry – you'll make yourself sick – come now – get up – do!

> *(His hands grasping her arms he half raises her to her feet, but, her face still hidden in her hands, sobbing, she slips on to his lap like a little girl and hides her face on his shoulder. His expression becomes transported with a great happiness.)*
> *(In an ecstatic whisper.)*

As I dreamed . . . with a deeper sweetness! . . .

> *(He kisses her hair with a great reverence.)*

There . . . this is all my desire . . . I am this kind of lover . . . this is my love . . . she is my girl . . . not woman . . . my little girl , . and I am brave because of her little girl's pure love . . . and I am proud . . . no more afraid . . . no more ashamed of being pure! . . .

> *(He kisses her hair again tenderly and smiles at himself.)*
> *(Then soothingly with a teasing incongruous gaiety.)*

This will never do, Nina Cara Nina — never, never do, you know — I can't permit it!

NINA

(*In a muffled voice, her sobbing beginning to ebb away into sighs — in a young girl's voice.*)

Oh, Charlie, you're so kind and comforting! I've wanted you so!

MARSDEN

(*Immediately disturbed.*)
Wanted? . . . wanted? . . . not that kind of wanted . . can she mean? . . .
(*Questioning hesitatingly.*)

You've wanted me, Nina?

NINA

Yes, — awfully! I've been so homesick. I've wanted to run home and 'fess up, tell how bad I've been, and be punished! Oh, I've got to be punished, Charlie, out of mercy for me, so I can forgive myself! And now Father dead, there's only you. You will, won't you — or tell me how to punish myself? You've simply got to, if you love me!

MARSDEN

(*Thinking intensely.*)
If I love her! . . oh, I do love her! . . .
(*Eagerly.*)

Anything you wish, Nina — anything!

78

NINA

(*With a comforted smile, closing her eyes and cuddling up against him.*)

I knew you would. Dear old Charlie!

(*As he gives a wincing start.*)

What is it?

(*She looks up into his face.*)

MARSDEN

(*Forcing a smile – ironically.*)

Twinge – rheumatics – getting old, Nina.

(*Thinking with wild agony.*)
Dear old Charlie! . . . descended again into hell! . . .
(*Then in a flat voice.*)

What do you want to be punished for, Nina?

NINA

(*In a strange, far-away tone, looking up not at him but at the ceiling.*)

For playing the silly slut, Charlie. For giving my cool clean body to men with hot hands and greedy eyes which they called love! Ugh!

(*A shiver runs over her body.*)

MARSDEN

(*Thinking with sudden agony.*)
Then she did! . . . the little filth! . . .
(*In his flat voice.*)

You mean you –

(*Then pleadingly.*)

But not – Darrell?

NINA

(*With simple surprise.*)

Ned? No, how could I? The war hadn't maimed him.
There would have been no point in that. But I did with
others – oh, four or five or six or seven men, Charlie. I forget – and it doesn't matter. They were all the same. Count
them all as one, and that one a ghost of nothing. That is, to
me. They were important to themselves, if I remember
rightly. But I forget.

MARSDEN

(*Thinking in agony.*)
But why? . . . the dirty little trollop! . . . why? . . .
(*In his flat voice.*)

Why did you do this, Nina?

NINA

(*With a sad little laugh.*)

God knows, Charlie! Perhaps I knew at the time, but I've
forgotten. It's all mixed up. There was a desire to be kind.
But it's horribly hard to give anything, and frightful to
receive! And to give love – oneself – not in this world! And
men are difficult to please, Charlie. I seemed to feel Gordon
standing against a wall with eyes bandaged and these men

were a firing squad whose eyes were also bandaged – and only I could see! No, I was the blindest! I would not see! I knew it was a stupid, morbid business, that I was more maimed than they were, really, that the war had blown my heart and insides out! And I knew too that I was torturing these tortured men, morbidly supersensitive already, that they loathed the cruel mockery of my gift! Yet I kept on, from one to one, like a stupid, driven animal until one night not long ago I had a dream of Gordon diving down out of the sky in flames and he looked at me with such sad burning eyes, and all my poor maimed men, too, seemed staring out of his eyes with a burning pain, and I woke up crying, my own eyes burning. Then I saw what a fool I'd been – a guilty fool! So be kind and punish me!

MARSDEN

(*Thinking with bitter confusion.*)

I wish she hadn't told me this . . . it has upset me terribly! . . . I positively must run home at once . . . Mother is waiting up . . . oh, how I'd love to hate this little whore! . . . then I could punish! . . . I wish her father were alive . . . "now he's dead there's only you," she said . . . "I've wanted you" . . .

(*With intense bitterness.*)

Dear old Father Charlie now! . . . ha! . . . that's how she wants me! . . .

(*Then suddenly in a matter-of-fact tone that is mockingly like her father's.*)

Then, under the circumstances, having weighed the pros and cons, so to speak, I should say that decidedly the most desirable course –

81

NINA

(Drowsily – her eyes shut.)

You sound so like Father, Charlie.

MARSDEN

(In the tone like her father's.)

– is for you to marry that young Evans. He is a splendid chap, clean and boyish, with real stuff in him, too, to make a career for himself if he finds a helpmate who will inspire him to his best efforts and bring his latent ability to the surface.

NINA

(Drowsily.)

Sam is a nice boy. Yes, it would be a career for me to bring a career to his surface. I would be busy – surface life – no more depths, please God! But I don't love him, Father.

MARSDEN

(Blandly – in the tone like her father's.)

But you like him, Nina. And he loves you devotedly. And it's time you were having children – and when children come, love comes, you know.

NINA

(Drowsily.)

I want children. I must become a mother so I can give myself. I am sick of sickness.

STRANGE INTERLUDE

MARSDEN

(*Briskly.*)

Then it's all settled?

NINA

(*Drowsily.*)

Yes.

(*Very sleepily.*)

Thank you, Father. You've been so kind. You've let me off too easily. I don't feel as if you'd punished me hardly at all. But I'll never, never do it again, I promise – never, never! –

(*She falls asleep and gives a soft little snore.*)

MARSDEN

(*Still in her father's tones – very paternally – looking down.*)

She's had a hard day of it, poor child! I'll carry her up to her room.

(*He rises to his feet with Nina sleeping peacefully in his arms. At this moment Sam Evans enters from the right with the package of medicine in his hand.*)

EVANS

(*Grinning respectfully.*)

Here's the –

(*As he sees Nina.*)

Oh!

(*Then excitedly.*)

Did she faint?

MARSDEN

(Smiling kindly at Evans – still in her father's tones.)

Sssh! She's asleep. She cried and then she fell asleep – like a little girl.

(Then benignantly.)

But first we spoke a word about you, Evans, and I'm sure you have every reason to hope.

EVANS

(Overcome, his eyes on his shuffling feet and twiddling cap.)

Thanks – I – I really don't know how to thank –

MARSDEN

(Going to door – in his own voice now.)

I've got to go home. My mother is waiting up for me. I'll just carry Nina upstairs and put her on her bed and throw something over her.

EVANS

Can't I help you, Mr. Marsden?

MARSDEN

(Dully.)

No. I cannot help myself.

(As Evans looks puzzled and startled he adds with an ironical, self-mocking geniality.)

You'd better call me just Charlie after this.

(He smiles bitterly to himself as he goes out.)

STRANGE INTERLUDE

*(Looks after him for a moment – then cannot restrain
a joyful, coltish caper – gleefully.)*

Good egg! Good old Charlie!

*(As if he had heard or guessed, Marsden's bitter
laugh comes back from the end of the hallway.)*

(Curtain.)

85

ACT THREE

SCENE: *Seven months or so later – the dining-room of the Evans'*
homestead in northern New York state – about nine o'clock
in the morning of a day in late spring of the following year.

The room is one of those big, misproportioned dining-
rooms that are found in the large, jigsaw country houses
scattered around the country as a reult of the rural taste for
grandeur in the 'eighties. There is a cumbersome hanging
lamp suspended from chains over the exact centre of the ugly
table with its set of straight-backed chairs set back at
spaced intervals against the walls. The wall-paper, a
repulsive brown, is stained at the ceiling line with damp
blotches of mildew, and here and there has started to peel
back where the strips join. The floor is carpeted in a
smeary brown with a dark red design blurred into it. In
the left wall is one window with starched white curtains
looking out on a covered side porch, so that no sunlight ever
gets to this room, and the light from the window, although
it is a beautiful warm day in the flower garden beyond the
porch, is cheerless and sickly. There is a door in the
rear, to left of centre, that leads to a hall opening
on the same porch. To the right of door a heavy side-
board, a part of the set, displaying some "company" china
and glassware. In the right wall, a door leading to the
kitchen.

Nina is seated at the foot of the table, her back to the
window, writing a letter. Her whole personality seems
changed, her face has a contented expression, there is an
inner calm about her. And her personal appearance has
changed in kind, her face and figure have filled out, she is
prettier in a conventional way and less striking and

unusual; nothing remains of the strange fascination of he
face except her unchangeably mysterious eyes.

NINA

(*Reading over to herself what she has just written.*)
It's a queer house, Ned. There is something wrong with
its psyche, I'm sure. Therefore you'd simply adore it.
It's a hideous old place, a faded gingerbread with orange
fixin's and numerous lightning rods. Around it are acres
and acres of apple trees in full bloom, all white and pinkish
and beautiful, like brides just tripping out of church with
the bridegroom, Spring, by the arm.

Which reminds me, Ned, that it's over six months since
Sam and I were married and we haven't seen hide nor hair
of you since the ceremony. Do you think that is any nice
way to act? You might at least drop me a line. But I'm
only joking. I know how busy you must be now that you've
got the chance: you've always wanted to do research work.
Did you get our joint letter of congratulation written after
we read of your appointment?

But to get back to this house. I feel it has lost its soul and
grown resigned to doing without it. It isn't haunted by
anything at all – and ghosts of some sort are the only normal
life a house has – like our minds, you know. So although
last evening when we got here at first I said "obviously
haunted" to myself, now that I've spent one night in it I
know that whatever spooks there may once have been have
packed up their manifestations a long time ago and
drifted away over the grass, wisps of mist between the
apple trees, without one backward glance of regard or recol-
lection. It's incredible to think Sam was born and spent his
childhood here. I'm glad he doesn't show it! We slept last
night in the room he was born in. Or rather he slept, I
couldn't. I lay awake and found it difficult to breathe, as if
all the life in the air had long since been exhausted in
keeping the dying living a little longer. It was hard to
believe anyone had ever been born alive there. I know

you're saying crossly "She's still morbid," but I'm not. I've never been more normal. I feel contented and placid.

(*Looking up from the letter, thinking embarrassedly.*)

Should I have told him? . . . no . . . my own secret . . . tell no one . . . not even Sam . . . why haven't I told Sam? . . . it'd do him much good . . . he'd feel so proud of himself, poor dear . . . no . . . I want to keep it just my baby . . . only mine . . . as long as I can . . . and it will be time enough to let Ned know when I go to New York . . . he can suggest a good obstetrician . . how delighted he'll be when he hears! . . . he always said it would be the best thing for me . . . well, I do feel happy when I think . . . and I love Sam now . . . in a way . . . it will be his baby too . . .

(*Then with a happy sigh, turns back to letter.*)

But speaking of Sam's birth, you really must meet his mother some time. It's amazing how little she is like him, a strange woman from the bit I saw of her last night. She has been writing Sam regularly once a week ever since she's known we were married, the most urgent invitations to visit her. They were really more like commands, or prayers. I suspect she is terribly lonely all by herself in this big house. Sam's feeling toward her puzzles me. I don't believe he ever mentioned her until her letters began coming or that he'd ever have come to see the poor woman if I hadn't insisted. His attitude rather shocked me. It was just as though he'd forgotten he had a mother. And yet as soon as he saw her he was sweet enough She seemed dreadfully upset to see Charlie with us, until we'd explained it was thanks to his kindness and in his car we were taking this deferred honeymoon. Charlie's like a fussy old woman about his car, he's afraid to let Sam or me drive it –

MARSDEN

(*Enters from the rear. He is spruce, dressed immaculately, his face a bit tired and resigned, but smiling kindly. He has a letter in his hand.*)

Good morning.

> (*She gives a start and instinctively covers the letter
> with her hand.*)

NINA

Good morning.

> (*Thinking amusedly.*)
> If he knew what I'd just written . . . poor old Char-
> lie! . . .
> (*Then indicating the letter he carries.*)

I see you're an early correspondent, too.

MARSDEN

> (*With sudden jealous suspicion.*)
> Why did she cover it up like that? . . . who's she
> writing to? . . .
> (*Coming toward her.*)

Just a line to Mother to let her know we've not all been
murdered by rum-bandits. You know how she worries.

NINA

> (*Thinking with a trace of pitying contempt.*)
> Apron strings . . . still his devotion to her is touching
> . . . I hope if mine is a boy he will love me as much . . .
> oh, I hope it is a boy . . . healthy and strong and beautiful
> . . . like Gordon! . . .
> (*Then suddenly sensing Marsden's curiosity – perfunc-
> torily.*)

I'm writing to Ned Darrell. I've owed him one for ages.

> (*She folds it up and puts it aside.*)

MARSDEN

(*Thinking glumly.*)
I thought she'd forgotten him . . . still, I suppose it's just friendly . . . and it's none of my business now she's married. . . .
(*Perfunctorily.*)

How did you sleep?

NINA

Not a wink. I had the strangest feeling.

MARSDEN

Sleeping in a strange bed, I suppose.
(*Jokingly.*)

Did you see any ghosts?

NINA

(*With a sad smile.*)

No, I got the feeling the ghosts had all deserted the house and left it without a soul – as the dead so often leave the living –

(*She forces a little laugh.*)

if you get what I mean.

MARSDEN

(*Thinking worriedly.*)
Slipping back into that morbid tone . . . first time in a long while . . .
(*Teasingly.*)

Hallo! Do I hear graveyards yawning from their sleep –
and yet I observe it's a gorgeous morning without, the
flowers are flowering, the trees are treeing with one another,
and you, if I mistake not, are on your honeymoon!

NINA

(*Immediately gaily mocking.*)

Oh, very well, old thing! "God's in his heaven, all's right
with the world!" And Pippa's cured of the pip!

(*She dances up to him.*)

MARSDEN

(*Gallantly.*)

Pippa is certainly a pippin this morning!

NINA

(*Kisses him quickly.*)

You deserve one for that! All I meant was that ghosts
remind me of men's smart crack about women, you can't live
with them and can't live without them.

(*Stands still and looks at him teasingly.*)

But there you stand proving me a liar by every breath you
draw! You're ghostless and womanless – and as sleek and
satisfied as a pet seal!

(*She sticks out her tongue at him and makes a face of
superior scorn.*)

Bah! That for you, 'Fraid-cat Charlie, you slacker
bachelor!

(*She runs to the kitchen door.*)

I'm going to bum some more coffee! How about you?

MARSDEN

(*With a forced smile.*)

No, thank you.

(*She disappears into the kitchen.*)
(*Thinking with bitter pain.*)

Ghostless! . . . if she only knew . . . that joking tone hides her real contempt! . . .

(*Self-mockingly.*)

"But when the girls began to play 'Fraid-cat Charlie ran away!"

(*Then rallying himself.*)

Bosh! . . . I haven't had such thoughts . . . not since their marriage . . . happy in her happiness . . . but is she happy? . . . in the first few months she was obviously playing a part . . . kissed him too much . . . as if she'd determined to make herself a loving wife . . . and then all of a sudden she became contented . . . her face filled out . . . her eyes lazily examined peace . . . pregnant . . . yes, she must be . . . I hope so . . . why? . . . for her sake . . . my own, too . . . when she has a child I know I can entirely accept . . . forget I have lost her . . . lost her? . . . silly ass! . . . how can you lose what you never possessed? . . . except in dreams! . . .

(*Shaking his head exasperatedly.*)

Round and round . . . thoughts . . . damn pests! . . . mosquitoes of the soul . . . whine, sting, suck one's blood . . . why did I invite Nina and Sam on this tour . . . it's a business trip with me, really . . . I need a new setting for my next novel . . . "Mr. Marsden departs a bit from his familiar field" . . . well, there they were stuck in the Professor's house . . couldn't afford a vacation . . . never had a honeymoon . . . I've pretended to be done up every night so they could . . . I've gone to bed right after dinner so they could be alone and . . . I wonder if she can really like him . . . that way? . . .

(*The sound of Evans' voice and his mother's is heard from the garden. Marsden goes over and carefully peers out.*)

Sam with his mother . . . peculiar woman . . . strong . . . good character for a novel . . . no, she's too sombre . . . her eyes are the saddest . . . and, at the same time, the grimmest . . . they're coming in . . . I'll drive around the country a bit . . . give them a chance for a family conference . . . discuss Nina's pregnancy, I suppose . . . does Sam know? . . . he gives no indication . . . why do wives hide it from their husbands? . . . ancient shame . . . guilty of continuing life, of bringing fresh pain into the world . . .

(*He goes out, rear. The outside door in the hall is heard being opened and Evans and his mother evidently meet Marsden as he is about to go out. Their voices, his voice explaining, are heard, then the outer door being opened and shut again as Marsden departs. A moment later Evans and his mother enter the dining-room. Sam looks timorously happy, as if he could not quite believe in his good fortune and had constantly to reassure himself about it, yet he is riding the crest of the wave, he radiates love and devotion and boyish adoration. He is a charming-looking fresh boy now. He wears a sweater and linen knickers, collegiate to the last degree. His mother is a tiny woman with a frail figure, her head and face, framed in iron-grey hair, seeming much too large for her body, so that at first glance she gives one the impression of a wonderfully made, life-like doll. She is only about forty-five, but she looks at least sixty. Her face with its delicate features must have once been of a romantic, tender, clinging-vine beauty, but what has happened to her has compressed its defenceless curves into planes, its mouth into the thin line around a locked door, its gentle chin has been forced out aggressively by a long reliance on*)

93

*clenched teeth. She is very pale. Her big dark
eyes are grim with the prisoner-pain of a walled-
in soul. Yet a sweet lovingkindness, the ghost
of an old faith and trust in life's goodness,
hovers girlishly, fleetingly, about the corners of
her mouth and softens into deep sorrow the
shadowy grimness of her eyes. Her voice jumps
startlingly in tone from a caressing gentleness to
a blunted flat assertiveness, as if what she said
then was merely a voice on its own without
human emotion to inspire it.)*

EVANS

*(As they come in – rattling on in the cocksure boastful
way of a boy showing off his prowess before his
mother, confident of thrilled adulation.)*

In a few years you won't have to worry one way or another
about the darned old apple crop. I'll be able to take care of
you then. Wait and see! Of course, I'm not making so
much now. I couldn't expect to. I've only just started. But
I'm making good, all right, all right – since I got married –
and it's only a question of time when – Why, to show you,
Cole – he's the manager and the best egg ever – called me
into his office and told me he'd had his eye on me, that my
stuff was exactly what they wanted, and he thought I had
the makings of a real find.

(Proudly.)

How's that? That's certainly fair enough, isn't it?

MRS. EVANS

*(Vaguely – she has evidently not heard much of what
he said.)*

That's fine, Sammy.

(Thinking apprehensively.)

94

I do hope I'm wrong! . . . but that old shiver of dread took me the minute she stepped in the door! . . . I don't think she's told Sammy, but I got to make sure. . . .

EVANS

(Seeing her preoccupation now – deeply hurt – testily.)

I'll bet you didn't hear a word I said! Are you still worrying about how the darn old apples are going to turn out?

MRS. EVANS

(With a guilty start – protestingly.)

Yes, I did hear you, Sammy – every word! That's just what I was thinking about – how proud I am you're doing so wonderful well!

EVANS

(Mollified but still grumbling.)

You'd never guess it from the gloomy way you looked!

(But encouraged to go on.)

And Cole asked me if I was married – seemed to take a real personal interest – said he was glad to hear it because marriage was what put the right kind of ambition into a fellow – unselfish ambition – working for his wife and not just himself –

(Then embarrassedly.)

He even asked me if we were expecting an addition to the family.

95

MRS. EVANS

(*Seeing this is her chance – quickly – forcing a smile.*)

I've been meaning to ask you that myself, Sammy.

(*Blurts out apprehensively.*)

She – Nina – she isn't going to have a baby, is she?

EVANS

(*With an indefinable guilty air – as if he were reluctant to admit it.*)

I – why – you mean, is she now? I don't think so, Mother.

(*He strolls over the window whistling with an exaggeratedly casual air, and looks out.*)

MRS. EVANS

(*Thinking with grim relief.*)

He don't know . . there's that much to be thankful for, anyway. . . .

EVANS

(*Thinking with intense longing.*)

If that'd only happen! . . . soon! . . . Nina's begun to love me . . . a little . . . I've felt it the last two months . . . God, it's made me happy! . . . before that she didn't . . only liked me . . . that was all I asked . . . never dared hope she'd come to love me . . . even a little . . . so soon . . . sometimes I feel it's too good to be true . . . don't deserve it . . . and now . . . if that'd happen . . . then I'd feel sure . . . it'd be there . . . half Nina, half me . . . living proof! . . .

(*Then an apprehensive note creeping in.*)

And I know she wants a baby so much . . . one reason

96

why she married me . . . and I know she's felt right along
that then she'd love me . . . really love me . . .

(*Gloomily.*)

I wonder why . . . ought to have happened before this
. . . hope it's nothing wrong . . . with me! . . .

(*He starts, flinging off this thought – then suddenly
clutching at a straw, turns hopefully to his
mother.*)

Why did you ask me that, Mother? D'you think – ?

MRS. EVANS

(*Hastily.*)

No, indeed! I don't think she is! I wouldn't say so at all!

EVANS

(*Dejectedly.*)

Oh – I thought perhaps –

(*Then changing the subject.*)

I suppose I ought to go up and say hallo to Aunt Bessie.

MRS. EVANS

(*Her face becoming defensive – in blunted tones, a
trifle pleadingly.*)

I wouldn't, Sammy. She hasn't seen you since you were
eight. She wouldn't know you. And you're on your honeymoon, and old age is always sad to young folks. Be happy
while you can!

(*Then pushing him toward door.*)

Look here! You catch that friend, he's just getting his car
out. You drive to town with him, give me a chance to get to

97

D

know my daughter-in-law, and call her to account for how she's taking care of you!

(*She laughs forcedly.*)

EVANS

(*Bursting out passionately.*)

Better than I deserve! She's an angel, Mother! I know you'll love her!

MRS. EVANS

(*Gently.*)

I do already, Sammy! She's so pretty and sweet!

EVANS

(*Kisses her – joyously.*)

I'll tell her that. I'm going out this way and kiss her good-bye.

(*He runs out through the kitchen door.*)

MRS. EVANS

(*Looking after him – passionately.*)

He loves her! . . . he's happy! . . . that's all that counts! . . . being happy! . . .

(*Thinking apprehensively.*)

If only she isn't going to have a baby . . . if only she doesn't care so much about having one . . I got to have it out with her . . . got to! . . . no other way . . . in mercy . . . in justice . . . this has got to end with my boy . . . and he's got to live happy! . . .

(*At the sound of steps from the kitchen she straightens up in her chair stiffly.*)

98

NINA

(*Comes in from the kitchen, a cup of coffee in her hand, smiling happily.*)

Good morning –

(*She hesitates – then shyly.*)

Mother.

(*She comes over and kisses her – slips down and sits on the floor beside her.*)

MRS. EVANS

(*Flusteredly – hurriedly.*)

Good morning! It's a real fine day, isn't it? I ought to have been here and got your breakfast, but I was out gallivanting round the place with Sammy. I hope you found everything you wanted.

NINA

Indeed I did! And I ate so much I'm ashamed of myself!

(*She nods at the cup of coffee and laughs.*)

See, I'm still at it!

MRS. EVANS

Good for you!

NINA

I ought to apologize for coming down so late. Sam should have called me. But I wasn't able to get to sleep until after daylight somehow.

MRS. EVANS

(Strangely.)

You couldn't sleep? Why? Did you feel anything funny — about this house?

NINA

(Struck by her tone – looks up.)

No. Why?

(Thinking.)
How her face changes! . . . what sad eyes! . . .

MRS. EVANS

(Thinking in an agony of apprehension.)
Got to start in to tell her . . got to . . .

NINA

(Apprehensive herself now.)
That sick dead feeling . . . when something is going to happen . . . I felt it before I got the cable about Gordon . . .

(Then taking a sip of coffee, and trying to be pleasantly casual.)

Sam said you wanted to talk to me.

MRS. EVANS

(Dully.)
Yes. You love my boy, don't you?

STRANGE INTERLUDE

NINA

(*Startled – forcing a smile, quickly.*)

Why, of course!

(*Reassuring herself.*)
No, it isn't a lie . . I do love him . . . the father of my baby . . .

MRS. EVANS

(*Blurts out.*)

Are you going to have a baby, Nina?

NINA

(*She presses Mrs. Evans' hand.*)
(*Simply.*)

Yes, Mother.

MRS. EVANS

(*In her blunt flat tones – with a mechanical rapidity to her words.*)

Don't you think it's too soon? Don't you think you better wait until Sammy's making more money? Don't you think it'll be a drag on him and you? Why don't you just go on being happy together, just you two?

NINA

(*Thinking frightenedly.*)
What is behind what she's saying? . . . that feeling of death again! . . .
(*Moving away from her – repulsed.*)

No, I don't think any of those things, Mrs. Evans. I want a baby – beyond everything! We both do!

MRS. EVANS

(*Hopelessly.*)

I know.

(*Then grimly.*)

But you can't! You've got to make up your mind you can't!

(*Thinking fiercely – even with satisfaction.*)
Tell her! . . . make her suffer what I was made to suffer!
. . . I've been too lonely! . . .

NINA

(*Thinking with terrified foreboding.*)
I knew it! . . . Out of a blue sky . . . black! . . .
(*Springing to her feet – bewilderedly.*)

What do you mean? How can you say a thing like that?

MRS. EVANS

(*Reaching out her hand tenderly, trying to touch Nina.*)

It's because I want Sammy – and you, too, child – to be happy.

(*Then as Nina shrinks away from her hand – in her blunted tones.*)

You just can't.

NINA

(*Defiantly.*)

But I can! I have already! I mean – I am, didn't you understand me?

MRS. EVANS

(*Gently.*)

I know it's hard.

(*Then inexorably.*)

But you can't go on!

NINA

(*Violently.*)

I don't believe you know what you're saying! It's too terrible for you – Sam's own mother – how would you have felt if someone – when you were going to have Sam – came to you and said –?

MRS. EVANS

(*Thinking fiercely.*)
Now's my chance! . . .
(*Tonelessly.*)

They did say it! Sam's own father did – my husband! And I said it to myself! And I did all I could, all my husband could think of, so's I wouldn't – but we didn't know enough. And right to the time the pains come on, I prayed Sammy'd be born dead, and Sammy's father prayed, but Sammy was born healthy and smiling, and we just had to love him, and live in fear. He doubled the torment of fear we lived in. And that's what you'd be in for. And Sammy, he'd go the way his father went. And your baby, you'd be bringing it into torment.

(*A bit violently.*)

I tell you it'd be a crime – a crime worse than murder!

(*Then recovering – commiseratingly.*)

So you just can't, Nina!

NINA

(*Who has been listening distractedly – thinking.*)
Don't listen to her! . . . feeling of death! . . . what is it?
. . . she's trying to kill my baby! . . . oh, I hate her! . . .
(*Hysterically resentful.*)

What do you mean? Why don't you speak plainly?

(*Violently.*)

I think you're horrible! Praying your baby would be
born dead! That's a lie! You couldn't!

MRS. EVANS

(*Thinking.*)
I know what she's doing now . . . just what I did . . .
trying not to believe . . .
(*Fiercely.*)
But I'll make her! . . . she's got to suffer, too! . . . I
been too lonely! . . . she's got to share and help me save
my Sammy! . . .
(*With an even more blunted flat relentless toneless-
ness.*)

I thought I was plain, but I'll be plainer. Only remember
it's a family secret, and now you're one of the family. It's
the curse on the Evanses. My husband's mother – she was
an only child – died in an asylum, and her father before her.
I know that for a fact. And my husband's sister, Sammy's
aunt, she's out of her mind. She lives on the top floor of this
house, hasn't been out of her room in years, I've taken care
of her. She just sits, doesn't say a word, but she's happy, she
laughs to herself a lot, she hasn't a care in the world. But I
remember when she was all right, she was always unhappy,
she never got married, most people around here were afraid of
the Evanses in spite of their being rich for hereabouts. They

knew about the craziness going back, I guess, for heaven knows how long. I didn't know about the Evanses until after I'd married my husband. He came to the town I lived in, no one there knew about the Evanses. He didn't tell me until after we were married. He asked me to forgive him, he said he loved me so much he'd have gone mad without me, said I was his only hope of salvation. So I forgave him. I loved him an awful lot. I said to myself, I'll be his salvation – and maybe I could have been if we hadn't had Sammy born. My husband kept real well up to then. We'd swore we'd never have children, we never forgot to be careful for two whole years. Then one night we'd both gone to a dance, we'd both had a little punch to drink, just enough – to forget – driving home in the moonlight – that moonlight! – such little things at the back of big things!

NINA

(*In a dull moan.*)

I don't believe you! I won't believe you!

MRS. EVANS

(*Drones on.*)

My husband, Sammy's father, in spite of all he and I fought against it, he finally gave in to it when Sammy was only eight, he couldn't keep up any more living in fear for Sammy, thinking any minute the curse might get him, every time he was sick, or had a headache, or bumped his head, or started crying, or had a nightmare and screamed, or said something queer like children do naturally.

(*A bit stridently.*)

Living like that with that fear is awful torment! I know

105

that! I went through it by his side! It nearly drove me crazy, too – but I didn't have it in my blood! And that's why I'm telling you! You got to see you can't, Nina!

NINA

(*Suddenly breaking out – frenziedly.*)

I don't believe you! I don't believe Sam would ever have married me if he knew – !

MRS. EVANS

(*Sharply.*)

Who said Sammy knew? He don't know a single thing about it! That's been the work of my life, keeping him from knowing. When his father gave up and went off into it I sent Sammy right off to boarding school. I told him his father was sick, and a little while after I sent word his father was dead, and from then on until his father did really die during Sammy's second year to college, I kept him away at school in winter and camp in summers and I went to see him, I never let him come home.

(*With a sigh.*)

It was hard, giving up Sammy, knowing I was making him forget he had a mother. I was glad taking care of them two kept me so busy I didn't get much chance to think then. But here's what I've come to think since, Nina: I'm certain sure my husband might have kept his mind with the help of my love if I hadn't had Sammy. And if I'd never had Sammy I'd never have loved Sammy – or missed him, would I? – and I'd have kept my husband.

NINA

(*Not heeding this last – with wild mockery.*)

And I thought Sam was so normal – so healthy and sane – not like me! I thought he'd give me such healthy, happy children and I'd forget myself in them and learn to love him!

MRS. EVANS

(*Horrified, jumping to her feet.*)

Learn to? You told me you did love Sammy!

NINA

No! Maybe I almost have – lately – but only when I thought of his baby! Now I hate him!

(*She begins to weep hysterically. Mrs. Evans goes to her and puts her arms around her. Nina sobs out.*)

Don't touch me! I hate you, too! Why didn't you tell him he must never marry?

MRS. EVANS

What reason could I give, without telling him everything? And I never heard about you till after you were married. Then I wanted to write to you, but I was scared he might read it. And I couldn't leave her upstairs to come away to see you. I kept writing Sammy to bring you here right off, although having him come frightened me to death for fear he might get to suspect something. You got to get him right away from here, Nina! I just kept hoping you wouldn't want children right away – young folks don't nowadays – until I'd seen you and told you everything. And I thought you'd love him like I did his father, and be satisfied with him alone.

NINA

(*Lifting her head – wildly.*)

No! I don't! I won't! I'll leave him!

MRS. EVANS

(*Shaking her – fiercely.*)

You can't! He'd go crazy sure then! You'd be a devil! Don't you see how he loves you?

NINA

(*Breaking away from her – harshly.*)

Well, I don't love him! I only married him because he needed me – and I needed children! And now you tell me I've got to kill my – oh, yes, I see I've got to, you needn't argue any more! I love it too much to make it run that chance! And I hate it too, now, because it's sick, it's not my baby, it's his!

(*With terrible ironic bitterness.*)

And still you can dare to tell me I can't even leave Sam!

MRS. EVANS

(*Very sadly and bitterly.*)

You just said you married him because he needed you. Don't he need you now – more'n ever? But I can't tell you not to leave him, not if you don't love him. But you oughtn't to have married him when you didn't love him. And it'll be your fault, what'll happen.

NINA

(*Torturedly.*)

What will happen? – what do you mean? – Sam will be all right – just as he was before – and it's not my fault, anyway! – it's not my fault!

(*Then thinking conscience-strickenly.*)

Poor Sam . . . she's right . . . it's not his fault . . . it's mine . . . I wanted to use him to save myself . . . I acted the coward again . . . as I did with Gordon . . .

MRS. EVANS

(*Grimly.*)

You know what'll happen to him if you leave him – after all I've told you!

(*Then breaking into intense pleading.*)

Oh, I'd get down on my knees to you, don't make my boy run that risk! You got to give one Evans, the last one, a chance to live in this world! And you'll learn to love him, if you give up enough for him!

(*Then with a grim smile.*)

Why, I even love that idiot upstairs, I've taken care of her so many years, lived her life for her with my life, you might say. You give your life to Sammy, then you'll love him same as you love yourself. You'll have to! That's sure as death!

(*She laughs a queer gentle laugh full of amused bitterness.*)

NINA

(*With a sort of dull stupid wonderment.*)

And you've found peace? –

MRS. EVANS

(*Sardonically.*)

There's peace in the green fields of Eden, they say! You got to die to find out!

(*Then proudly.*)

But I can say I feel proud of having lived fair to them that gave me love and trusted in me!

NINA

(*Struck – confusedly.*)

Yes – that's true, isn't it?

(*Thinking strangely.*)

Lived fair . . . pride . . . trust . . . play the game! . . who is speaking to me . . . Gordon! . . . oh, Gordon, do you mean I must give Sam the life I didn't give you? . . . Sam loved you, too . . . he said, if we have a boy, we'll call him Gordon in Gordon's honour . . . Gordon's honour! . . . what must I do now in your honour, Gordon? . . . yes! . . . I know! . . .

(*Speaking mechanically in a dull voice.*)

All right, Mother. I'll stay with Sam. There's nothing else I can do, is there, when it isn't his fault, poor boy!

(*Then suddenly snapping and bursting out in a despairing cry.*)

But I'll be so lonely! I'll have lost my baby!

(*She sinks down on her knees at Mrs. Evans' feet – piteously.*)

Oh, Mother, how can I keep on living?

MRS. EVANS

(*Thinking miserably.*)

Now she knows my suffering . . . now I got to help her
. . . she's got a right to have a baby . . . another baby
. . . sometime . . . somehow . . . she's giving her life to
save my Sammy . . . I got to save her! . . .

(*Stammeringly.*)

Maybe, Nina —

NINA

(*Dully and resentfully again now.*)

And how about Sam? You want him to be happy, don't
you? It's just as important for him as it is for me that I
should have a baby! If you know anything at all about him,
you ought to see that!

MRS. EVANS

(*Sadly.*)

I know that. I see that in him, Nina.

(*Gropingly.*)

There must be a way — somehow. I remember when I was
carrying Sam, sometimes I'd forget I was a wife, I'd only
remember the child in me. And then I used to wish I'd gone
out deliberate in our first year, without my husband knowing,
and picked a man, a healthy male to breed by, same's we do
with stock, to give the man I loved a healthy child. And if I
didn't love that other man nor him me where would be the
harm? Then God would whisper: "It'd be a sin, adultery,
the worst sin!" But after He'd gone I'd argue back again to
myself, then we'd have a healthy child, I needn't be afraid!
And maybe my husband would feel without ever knowing

III

how he felt it, that I wasn't afraid and that child wasn't cursed and so he needn't fear and I could save him.

(*Then scornfully.*)

But I was too afraid of God then to have ever done it!

(*Then very simply.*)

He loved children so, my poor husband did, and the way they took to him, you never saw anything like it, he was a natural born father. And Sammy's the same.

NINA

(*As from a distance – strangely.*)

Yes, Sammy's the same. But I'm not the same as you.

(*Defiantly.*)

I don't believe in God the Father!

MRS. EVANS

(*Strangely.*)

Then it'd be easy for you.

(*With a grim smile.*)

And I don't believe in Him, neither, not any more. I used to be a great one for worrying about what's God and what's devil, but I got richly over it living here with poor folks that was being punished for no sins of their own, and me being punished with them for no sin but loving much.

(*With decision.*)

Being happy, that's the nearest we can ever come to knowing what's good! Being happy, that's good! The rest is just talk!

(*She pauses – then with a strange austere sternness.*)

I love my boy, Sammy. I could see how much he wants you to have a baby. Sammy's got to feel sure you love him — to be happy. Whatever you can do to make him happy is good — is good, Nina! I don't care what! You've got to have a healthy baby — some time — so's you can both be happy! It's your rightful duty!

NINA

(*Confusedly — in a half-whisper.*)

Yes, Mother.

(*Thinking longingly.*)
I want to be happy! . . . it's my right . . . and my duty! . . .
(*Then suddenly in guilty agony.*)
Oh, my baby . . . my poor baby . . . I'm forgetting you . . desiring another after you are dead! . . . I feel you beating against my heart for mercy . . . oh! . .
(*She weeps with bitter anguish.*)

MRS. EVANS

(*Gently and with deep sympathy.*)

I know what you're suffering. And I wouldn't say what I just said now only I know us two mustn't see each other ever again. You and Sammy have got to forget me.

(*As Nina makes a motion of protest — grimly and inexorably.*)

Oh, yes, you will — easy. People forget everything. They got to, poor people! And I'm saying what I said about a healthy baby so's you will remember it when you need to, after you've forgotten — this one.

NINA

(*Sobbing pitifully.*)

Don't! Please, Mother!

MRS EVANS

(*With sudden tenderness – gathering Nina up in her
arms, brokenly.*)

You poor child! You're like the daughter of my sorrow!
You're closer to me now than ever Sammy could be! I want
you to be happy!

(*She begins to sob, too, kissing Nina's bowed head.*)

(*Curtain.*)

ACT FOUR

SCENE: *An evening early in the following winter about seven months later. The Professor's study again. The books in the cases have never been touched, their austere array shows no gaps, but the glass separating them from the world is grey with dust, giving them a blurred ghostly quality. The table, although it is the same, is no longer the Professor's table, just as the other furniture in the room, by its disarrangement, betrays that the Professor's well-ordered mind no longer trims it to his personality. The table has become neurotic. Volumes of the "Encyclopædia Britannica" mixed up with popular treatises on "Mind Training for Success," etc., looking startlingly modern and disturbing against the background of classics in the original, are slapped helter-skelter on top of each other on it. The titles of these books face in all directions, no one volume is placed with any relation to the one beneath it — the effect is that they have no connected meaning. The rest of the table is littered with an ink bottle, pens, pencils, erasers, a box of typewriting paper, and a typewriter at the centre before the chair, which is pushed back, setting the rug askew. On the floor beside the table are an overflowing waste paper basket, a few sheets of paper and the rubber cover for the typewriter like a collapsed tent. The rocking chair is no longer at centre but has been pulled nearer the table, directly faces it with its back to the bench. This bench in turn has been drawn much closer, but is now placed more to the rear and half faces front, its back squarely to the door in the corner.*

Evans is seated in the Professor's old chair. He has evidently been typing, or is about to type, for a sheet of

115

*paper can be seen in the machine. He smokes a pipe, which
he is always re-lighting whether it needs it or not, and
which he bites and shifts about and pulls in and out and
puffs at nervously. His expression is dispirited, his eyes
shift about, his shoulders are collapsed submissively. He
seems much thinner, his face drawn and sallow. The collegiate clothes are no longer natty, they need pressing and
look too big for him.*

EVANS

> (*Turns to his typewriter and pounds out a few words
> with a sort of aimless desperation – then tears
> the sheet out of the machine with an exclama-
> tion of disgust, crumples it up and throws it
> violently on the floor, pushing his chair back
> and jumping to his feet.*)

Hell!

> (*He begins pacing up and down the room, puffing at
> his pipe, thinking tormentedly.*)

No use . . . can't think of a darn thing . . . well, who
could dope out a novel ad on another powdered milk, anyway? . . . all the stuff been used already . . . Tartars con-
quering on dried mare's milk . . . Metchnikoff, eminent
scientist . . . been done to death . . . but simply got to
work out something or . . . Cole said, what's been the
matter with you lately? . . . you started off so well . . . I
thought you were a real find, but your work's fallen off to
nothing . . .

> (*He sits down on the edge of the bench near by, his
> shoulders hunched – despondently.*)

Couldn't deny it . . . been going stale ever since we came
back from that trip home . . . no ideas . . . I'll get fired
. . . sterile . . .

> (*With a guilty terror.*)

in more ways than one, I guess! . . .

(*He springs to his feet as if this idea were a pin stuck in him – lighting his already lighted pipe, walks up and down again, forcing his thoughts into other channels.*)

Bet the old man turns over in his grave at my writing ads in his study . . . maybe that's why I can't . . . bum influence . . . try to-morrow in my bedroom . . . sleeping alone . . . since Nina got sick . . . some woman's sickness . . . wouldn't tell me . . . too modest . . . still, there are some things a husband has a right to know . . . especially when we haven't . . . in five months . . . doctor told her she mustn't, she said . . . what doctor? . . . she's never said . . . what the hell's the matter with you, do you think Nina's lying? . . . no . . . but . . .

(*Desperately.*)

If I was only sure it was because she's really sick . . . not just sick of me! . . .

(*He sinks down in the rocking chair despondently.*)

Certainly been a big change in her . . . since that visit home . . . what happened between Mother and her? . . . she says nothing . . . they seemed to like each other . . . both of them cried when we left . . . still, Nina insisted on going that same day and Mother seemed anxious to get rid of us . . . can't make it out . . . next few weeks Nina couldn't be loving enough . . . I never was so happy . . . then she crashed . . . strain of waiting and hoping she'd get pregnant . . . and nothing happening . . . that's what did it . . . my fault! . . . how d'you know? . . . you can't tell that! . . .

(*He jumps to his feet again – walks up and down again distractedly.*)

God, if we'd only have a kid! . . . then I'd show them all what I could do! . . . Cole always used to say I had the stuff, and Ned certainly thought so. . . .

(*With sudden relieved excitement.*)

By gosh, I was forgetting! . . . Ned's coming out to-night . . . forgot to tell Nina . . . mustn't let her get wise I got him to come to look her over . . . she'd hate me for swal-

lowing my pride after he's never been to see us . . . but I
had to . . . this has got my goat . . . I've got to know what's
wrong . . . and Ned's the only one I can trust . . .

> (*He flings himself on chair in front of desk and, pick-
> ing up a fresh sheet of paper, jams it into the
> machine.*)

Gosh, I ought to try and get a new start on this before
it's time . . .

> (*He types a sentence or two, a strained frown of con-
> centration on his face. Nina comes silently
> through the door and stands just inside it looking
> at him. She has grown thin again, her face is
> pale and drawn, her movements are those of
> extreme nervous tension.*)

NINA

> (*Before she can stifle her immediate reaction of con-
> tempt and dislike.*)

How weak he is! . . . he'll never do anything . . . never
give me my desire . . . if he'd only fall in love with someone else . . . go away . . . not be here in my father's room
. . . I even have to give him a home . . . if he'd disappear
. . . leave me free . . . if he'd die . . .

> (*Checking herself – remorsefully.*)

I must stop such thoughts . . . I don't mean it . . . poor
Sam! . . . trying so hard . . . loving me so much . . . I
give so little in return . . . he feels I'm always watching
him with scorn . . . I can't tell him it's with pity . . . how
can I help watching him? . . . help worrying over his worry
because of what it might lead to . . . after what his mother
. . . how horrible life is! . . . he's worried now . . . he
doesn't sleep . . . I hear him tossing about . . . I must
sleep with him again soon . . . he's only home two nights a
week . . . it isn't fair of me . . . I must try . . I must!
. . . he suspects my revulsion . . . it's hurting him . . . oh,
poor dead baby I dared not bear, how I might have loved
your father for your sake! . . .

EVANS

(*Suddenly feeling her presence, jerks himself to his feet – with a diffident guilty air which is noticeable about him now whenever he is in her presence.*)

Hallo, dear! I thought you were lying down.

(*Guiltily.*)

Did the noise of my typing bother you? I'm terribly sorry!

NINA

(*Irritated in spite of herself.*)
Why is he always cringing? . . .
(*She comes forward to the chair at centre and sits down – forcing a smile.*)

But there's nothing to be terribly sorry about!

(*As he stands awkard and confused, like a schoolboy who has been called on to recite and cannot and is being "bawled out" before the class, she forces a playful tone.*)

Goodness, Sam, how tragic you can get about nothing at all!

EVANS

(*Still forced to justify himself – contritely.*)

I know it isn't pleasant for you having me drag my work out here, trying to pound out rotten ads.

(*With a short laugh.*)

Trying to is right!

(*Blurts out.*)

I wouldn't do it except that Cole gave me a warning to buck up – or get out.

NINA

*(Stares at him, more annoyed, her eyes hardening,
thinking.)*
Yes! . . . he'll always be losing one job, getting another,
starting with a burst of confidence each time, then . . .
(Cutting him with a careless sneering tone.)

Well, it isn't a job to worry much about losing, is it?

EVANS

(Wincing pitiably.)

No, not much money. But I used to think there was a fine
chance to rise there — but of course that's my fault, I haven't
made good —

(He finishes miserably.)

somehow.

NINA

(Her antagonism giving way to remorseful pity.)
What makes me so cruel? . . . he's so defenceless . . . his
mother's baby . . . poor sick baby! . . . poor Sam! . . .
(She jumps to her feet and goes over to him.)

EVANS

(As she comes – with a defensive, boastful bravery.)

Oh, I can get another job just as good, all right – maybe a
lot better.

NINA

(Reassuringly.)

Certainly, you can! And I'm sure you're not going to lose
this one. You're always anticipating trouble.

(She kisses him and sits on the arm of his chair, putting an arm around his neck and pulling his head on to her breast.)

And it isn't your fault, you big goose, you! It's mine. I know how hard it makes everything for you, being tied to a wife who's too sick to be a wife. You ought to have married a big strapping, motherly –

EVANS

(In the seventh heaven now – passionately.)

Bunk! All the other women in the world aren't worth your little finger! It's you who ought to have married some one worth while, not a poor fish like me! But no one could love you more than I do, no matter what he was!

NINA

(Presses his head on her breast, avoiding his eyes, kisses him on the forehead.)

And I love you, Sam.

(Staring out over his head – with loving pity, thinking.)

I almost do . . . poor unfortunate boy! . . . at these moments . . . as his mother loves him . . . but that isn't enough for him . . . I can hear his mother saying, "Sammy's got to feel sure you love him . . . to be happy." . . . I must try to make him feel sure . . .

(Speaking gently.)

I want you to be happy, Sam.

EVANS

(His face transformed with happiness.)

I am – a hundred times more than I deserve!

121

NINA

*(Presses his head down on her breast so he cannot see
her eyes – gently.)*

Ssshh!

(Thinking sadly.)

I promised her . . . but I couldn't see how hard it would
be to let him love me . . . after his baby . . . was gone
. . . it was hard even to keep on living . . . after that operation . . . Gordon's spirit followed me from room to room
. . . poor reproachful ghost! . . .

(With bitter mockery.)

Oh, Gordon, I'm afraid this is a deeper point of honour
than any that was ever shot down in flames! . . . what would
your honour say now? . . . "Stick to him! . . . play the
game!" . . . oh, yes, I know . . . I'm sticking . . . but he
isn't happy . . . I'm trying to play the game . . . then why
do I keep myself from him? . . . but I was really sick . . .
for a time after . . . since then, I couldn't . . . but . . .
oh, I'll try . . . I'll try soon . . .

(Tenderly – but having to force herself to say it.)

Doesn't my boy want to sleep with me again – some time
soon?

EVANS

(Passionately – hardly able to believe his ears.)

Oh, it'd be wonderful, Nina! But are you sure you really
want me to – that you'll feel well enough?

NINA

*(Repeats his words as if she were memorizing a
lesson.)*

Yes, I want you to. Yes, I'll feel well enough.

*(He seizes her hand and kisses it in a passionately
grateful silence.)*
(She thinks with resigned finality.)

There, Sammy's mother and Gordon . . . I'll play the game . . . it will make him happy for a while . . . as he was in those weeks after we'd left his mother . . . when I gave myself with a mad pleasure in torturing myself for his pleasure! . . .

(*Then with weary hopelessness.*)

He'll be happy until he begins to feel guilty again because I'm not pregnant . . .

(*With a grim bitter smile.*)

Poor Sam, if he only knew the precautions . . . as if I wouldn't die rather than take the slightest chance of that happening! . . . ever again . . . what a tragic joke it was on both of us! . . . I wanted my baby so! . . . oh, God! . . . his mother said . . . "You've got to have a healthy baby . . . some time . . . it's your rightful duty" . . . that seemed right then . . . but now . . . it seems cowardly . . . to betray poor Sam . . . and vile to give myself . . . without love or desire . . . and yet I've given myself to men before without a thought, just to give them a moment's happiness . . . can't I do that again? . . . when it's a case of Sam's happiness? . . . and my own? . . .

(*She gets up from beside him with a hunted movement.*)

It must be half-past eight. Charlie's coming to bring his suggestions on my outline for Gordon's biography.

EVANS

(*His bliss shattered – dejectedly.*)

Always happens . . . just as we get close . . . something comes between . . .

(*Then confusedly.*)

Say, I forgot to tell you Ned's coming out to-night.

NINA

(*Astonished.*)

Ned Darrell?

EVANS

Sure. I happened to run into him the other day and invited him and he said Saturday evening. He couldn't tell what train. Said never mind meeting him.

NINA

(*Excitedly.*)

Why didn't you tell me before, you big booby?

(*She kisses him.*)

There, don't mind. But it's just like you. Now someone'll have to go down to the store. And I'll have to get the spare room ready.

(*She hurries to the doorway. He follows her.*)

EVANS

I'll help you.

NINA

You'll do nothing of the kind! You'll stay right downstairs and bring them in here and cover up my absence. Thank heavens, Charlie won't stay long if Ned is here.

(*The door-bell rings – excitedly.*)

There's one of them now. I'll run upstairs. Come up and tell me if it's Ned – and get rid of Charlie.

(*She kisses him playfully and hurries out.*)

EVANS

(*Looking after her – thinks.*)

She seems better to-night . . . happier . . . she seems to

love me . . . if she'll only get all well again, then everything
will . . .

> (*The bell rings again.*)

I must give Ned a good chance to talk to her . . .

> (*He goes out to the outer door – returns a moment
> later with Marsden. The latter's manner is pre-
> occupied and nervous. His face has an expres-
> sion of anxiety which he tries to conceal. He
> seems a prey to some inner fear he is trying to
> hide even from himself and is resolutely warding
> off from his consciousness. His tall, thin body
> stoops as if a part of its sustaining will had
> been removed.*)

EVANS

> (*With a rather forced welcoming note.*)

Come on in, Charlie. Nina's upstairs lying down.

MARSDEN

> (*With marked relief.*)

Then by all means don't disturb her. I just dropped in to
bring back her outline with the suggestions I've made.

> (*He has taken some papers out of his pocket and
> hands them to Evans.*)

I couldn't have stayed but a minute in any event. Mother
is a bit under the weather these days.

EVANS

> (*Perfunctorily.*)

Too bad.

> (*Thinking vindictively.*)
> Serve her right, the old scandal-monger, after the way
> she's gossiped about Nina! . . .

MARSDEN

(*With assumed carelessness.*)

Just a little indigestion. Nothing serious, but it annoys her terribly.

(*Thinking frightenedly.*)
That dull pain she complains of . . . I don't like it . . . and she won't see anyone but old Doctor Tibbetts . . . she's sixty-eight . . . I can't help fearing . . no! . . .

EVANS

(*Bored – vaguely.*)

Well, I suppose you've got to be careful of every little thing when you get to her age.

MARSDEN

(*Positively bristling.*)

Her age? Mother isn't so old!

EVANS

(*Surprised.*)

Over sixty-five, isn't she?

MARSDEN

(*Indignantly.*)

You're quite out there! She's still under sixty-five – and in health and spirits she isn't more than fifty! Everyone remarks that!

(*Annoyed at himself.*)
Why did I lie to him about her age? . . . I must be on edge . . . Mother is rather difficult to live with these

days, getting me worried to death, when it's probably nothing . . .

EVANS

(*Annoyed in his turn – thinking.*)
Why all the fuss? . . . as if I gave a damn if the old girl was a million! . . .
(*Indicating the papers.*)

I'll give these to Nina first thing in the morning.

MARSDEN

(*Mechanically.*)
Right-o! Thank you.
(*He starts to go toward door – then turns – fussily.*)

But you'd better take a look while I'm here and see if it's clear. I've written on the margins. See if there's anything you can't make out.

(*Evans nods helplessly and begins reading the sheets, going back beneath the lamp.*)

MARSDEN

(*Looking around him with squeamish disapproval.*)
What a mess they've made of this study! . . . poor Professor! . . . dead and forgotten . . . and his tomb desecrated . . . does Sam write his ads here of a week-end now? . . . the last touch! . . . and Nina labours with love at Gordon's biography . . . whom the Professor hated! . . . "life is so full of a number of things!" . . . why does everyone in the world think they can write? . . . but I've only myself to blame . . . why the devil did I ever suggest it to her? . . . because I hoped my helping her while Sam was in the city would bring us alone together? . . . but I made the suggestion before she had that abortion performed! . . . how do you know she did? . . . because I know! . . . there

are psychic affinities . . . her body confessed . . . and since then, I've felt an aversion . . . as if she were a criminal . . she is! . . . how could she? . . . why? . . . I thought she wanted a child . . . but evidently I don't know her . . . I suppose, afraid it would spoil her figure . . . her flesh . . . her power to enslave men's senses . . . mine . . . and I had hoped . . . looked forward to her becoming a mother . . . for my peace of mind. . . .

(*Catching himself – violently.*)

Shut up! . . . what a base creature I'm becoming! . . . to have such thoughts when Mother is sick and I ought to be thinking only of her! . . . and it's none of my damn business, anyway! . . .

(*Glaring at Evans resentfully as if he were to blame.*)

Look at him! . . . he'll never suspect anything! . . . what a simple-simon! . . . he adored Gordon as a newsboy does a champion pugilist! . . . and Nina writes of Gordon as if he had been a demi-god! . . . when actually he came from the commonest people! . . .

(*He suddenly speaks to Evans with a really savage satisfaction.*)

Did I tell you I once looked up Gordon's family in Beach-ampton? A truly deplorable lot! When I remembered Gordon and looked at his father I had either to suspect a lover in the wood pile or to believe in an Immaculate Conception . . . that is, until I saw his mother! Then a stork became the only conceivable explanation!

EVANS

(*Who has only half heard and hasn't understood, says vaguely.*)

I never saw his folks.

(*Indicating the papers.*)

I can make this all out all right.

MARSDEN

(*Sarcastically.*)

I'm glad it's understandable!

EVANS

(*Blunderingly.*)

I'll give it to Nina – and I hope your mother is feeling better to-morrow.

MARSDEN

(*Piqued.*)

Oh, I'm going. Why didn't you tell me if I was interrupting – your writing!

EVANS

(*Immediately guilty.*)

Oh, come on, Charlie, don't get peevish, you know I didn't mean –

(*The bell rings. Evans stammers in confusion, trying at a nonchalant air.*)

Hallo! That must be Ned. You remember Darrell? He's coming out for a little visit. Excuse me.

(*He blunders out of the door.*)

MARSDEN

(*Looking after him with anger mixed with alarmed suspicion and surprise.*)

Darrell? . . . what's he doing here? . . . have they been meeting? . . . perhaps he was the one who performed the . . . no, his idea was she ought to have a child . . but if

129

E

she came and begged him? . . . but why should Nina beg not to have a baby? . . .

> (*Distractedly.*)

Oh, I don't know! . . . it's all a sordid mess! . . . I ought to be going home! . . . I don't want to see Darrell! . . .

> (*He starts for the door – then struck by a sudden thought, stops.*)

Wait . . . I could ask him about Mother . . . yes . . . good idea . . .

> (*He comes back to the middle of the room, front, and is standing there when Darrell enters, followed by Evans. Darrell has not changed in appearance except that his expression is graver and more thoughtful. His manner is more convincingly authoritative, more mature. He takes in Marsden from head to foot with one comprehensive glance.*)

EVANS

> (*Awkwardly.*)

Ned, you remember Charlie Marsden?

MARSDEN

> (*Holding out his hand, urbanely polite.*)

How are you, Doctor?

DARRELL

> (*Shaking his hand – briefly.*)

Hallo!

EVANS

I'll go up and tell Nina you're here, Ned.

> (*He goes, casting a resentful glance at Marsden.*)

MARSDEN

(*Awkwardly, as Darrell sits down in the chair at centre, goes over and stands by the table.*)

I was on the point of leaving when you rang. Then I decided to stop and renew our acquaintance.

(*He stoops and picks up one sheet of paper, and puts it back carefully on the table.*)

DARRELL

(*Watching him – thinking.*)

Neat . . . suspiciously neat . . . he's an old maid who seduces himself in his novels . . . so I suspect . . . I'd like a chance to study him more closely. . . .

MARSDEN

(*Thinking resentfully.*)

What a boor! . . . he might say something! . . .

(*Forcing a smile.*)

And I wanted to ask a favour of you, a word of advice as to the best specialist, the very best, it would be possible to consult –

DARRELL

(*Sharply.*)

On what?

MARSDEN

(*Almost naïvely.*)

My mother has a pain in her stomach.

DARRELL

(*Amused – dryly.*)

Possibly she eats too much.

MARSDEN

(*As he bends and carefully picks another sheet from the floor to place it as carefully on the table.*)

She doesn't eat enough to keep a canary alive. It's a dull, constant pain, she says. She's terribly worried. She's terrified by the idea of cancer. But, of course, that's perfect rot, she's never been sick a day in her life and –

DARRELL

(*Sharply.*)

She's showing more intelligence about her pain than you are.

MARSDEN

(*Bending down for another sheet, his voice trembling with terror.*)

I don't understand – quite. Do you mean to say you think – ?

DARRELL

(*Brutally.*)

It's possible.

(*He has pulled out his pen and a card and is writing.*)
(*Thinking grimly.*)
Explode a bomb under him, as I did once before . . . only way to get him started doing anything. . . .

MARSDEN

(*Angrily.*)

But – that's nonsense!

DARRELL

(*With satisfaction – unruffledly.*)

People who are afraid to face unpleasant possibilities until it's too late commit more murders and suicides than –

(*Holds out a card.*)

Doctor Schultz is your man. Take her to see him – tomorrow!

MARSDEN

(*Bursting out in anger and misery.*)

Damn it, you're condemning her without – !

(*He breaks down chokingly.*)

You've no damn right – !

(*He bends down, trembling all over, to pick up another piece of paper.*)

DARRELL

(*Genuinely astonished and contrite.*)
And I thought he was so ingrown he didn't care a damn about anyone! . . . his mother . . . now I begin to see him . . .
(*He jumps from his chair and going to Marsden puts a hand on his shoulder – kindly.*)

I beg your pardon, Marsden. I only wanted to drive it in that all delay is dangerous. Your mother's pain may be due to any number of harmless causes, but you owe it to her to make sure. Here.

(*He hands out the card.*)

MARSDEN

(*Straightens up and takes it, his eyes grateful now – humbly.*)

Thank you. I'll take her to see him to-morrow.

(*Evans comes in.*)

EVANS

(*To Marsden, blunderingly.*)

Say, Charlie, I don't want to hurry you, but Nina wants some things at the store before it closes, and if you'd give me a lift –

MARSDEN

(*Dully.*)

Of course. Come along.

(*He shakes hands with Darrell.*)

Good night, Doctor – and thank you.

DARRELL

Good night.

(*Marsden goes, followed by Evans.*)

EVANS

(*Turns in the doorway and says meaningly.*)

Nina'll be right down. For Pete's sake, have a good heart-to-heart talk with her, Ned!

DARRELL

(*Frowning – impatiently.*)

Oh – all right! Run along.

(*Evans goes.*)

> (*Darrell remains standing near the table looking after them, thinking about Marsden.*)

Queer fellow, Marsden . . mother's boy still . . . if she dies what will he do? . .

> (*Then dismissing Marsden with a shrug of his shoulders.*)

Oh, well, he can always escape life in a new book. . . .

> (*He moves around the table examining its disorder critically, then sits down in arm-chair – amused.*)

Evidences of authorship . . . Sam's ads? . . . isn't making good, he said . . . was I wrong in thinking he had stuff in him? . . . hope not . . . always liked Sam, don't know why exactly . . . said Nina'd gotten into a bad state again . . . what's happened to their marriage? . . . I felt a bit sorry for myself at their wedding . . . not that I'd ever fallen . . . but I did envy him in a way . . . she always had strong physical attraction for me . . . that time I kissed her . . . one reason I've steered clear since . . . take no chances on emotional didos . . . need all my mind on my work . . . got rid of even that slight suspicion . . . I'd forgotten all about her . . . she's a strange girl . . . interesting case . . . I should have kept in touch on that account . . . hope she'll tell me about herself . . . can't understand her not having child . . . it's so obviously the sensible thing . . .

> (*Cynically.*)

Probably why . . . to expect common sense of people proves you're lacking in it yourself! . .

NINA

> (*Enters silently. She has fixed herself up, put on her best dress, arranged her hair, rouged, etc. – but it is principally her mood that has changed her, making her appear a younger, prettier person for the moment. Darrell immediately senses her presence, and, looking up, gets to his feet with a smile of affectionate admiration. She comes quickly over to him saying with frank pleasure:*)

Hallo, Ned! I'm certainly glad to see you again – after all these years!

DARRELL

(*As they shake hands – smiling.*)

Not as long as all that, is it?

(*Thinking admiringly.*)
Wonderful-looking as ever . . . Sam is a lucky devil! . . .

NINA

(*Thinking.*)
Strong hands like Gordon's . . . take hold of you . . . not like Sam's . . . yielding fingers that let you fall back into yourself . . .

(*Teasingly.*)

I ought to cut you dead after the shameful way you've ignored us!

DARRELL

(*A bit embarrassedly.*)

I've really meant to write.

(*His eyes examining her keenly.*)
Been through a lot since I saw her . . . face shows it . . . nervous tension pronounced . . . hiding behind her smile . . .

NINA

(*Uneasy under his glance.*)
I hate that professional look in his eyes . . . watching symptoms . . . without seeing me . . .

(*With resentful mockery.*)

136

Well, what do you suspect is wrong with the patient now, Doctor?

(*She laughs nervously.*)

Sit down, Ned. I suppose you can't help your diagnosing stare.

(*She turns from him and sits down in the rocker at centre.*)

DARRELL

(*Quickly averting his eyes – sits down – jokingly.*)

Same old unjust accusation! You were always reading diagnosis into me, when what I was really thinking was what fine eyes you had, or what a becoming gown, or –

NINA

(*Smiling.*)

Or what a becoming alibi you could cook up! Oh, I know you!

(*With a sudden change of mood she laughs gaily and naturally.*)

But you're forgiven – that is, if you can explain why you've never been to see us.

DARRELL

Honestly, Nina, I've been so rushed with work I haven't had a chance to go anywhere.

NINA

Or an inclination!

137

DARRELL

(*Smiling.*)

Well – maybe.

NINA

Do you like the Institute so much?

(*He nods gravely.*)

Is it the big opportunity you wanted?

DARRELL

(*Simply.*)

I think it is.

NINA

(*With a smile.*)

Well, you're the taking kind for whom opportunities are made!

DARRELL

(*Smiling.*)

I hope so.

NINA

(*Sighing.*)

I wish that could be said of more of us –

(*Then quickly.*)

– meaning myself.

DARRELL

(*Thinking with a certain satisfaction.*)

Meaning Sam . . . that doesn't look hopeful for future wedded bliss! . . .

(*Teasingly.*)

138

But I heard you were "taking an opportunity" to go in for
literature – collaborating with Marsden.

NINA

No, Charlie is only going to advise. He'd never deign to
appear as co-author. And, besides, he never appreciated the
real Gordon. No one did except me.

DARRELL

(*Thinking caustically.*)
Gordon myth strong as ever . . root of her trouble
still . . .
(*Keenly inquisitive.*)
Sam certainly appreciated him, didn't he?

NINA

(*Not remembering to hide her contempt.*)
Sam? Why, he's the exact opposite in every way!

DARRELL

(*Caustically thinking.*)
These heroes die hard . . . but perhaps she can write
him out of her system. . . .
(*Persuasively.*)
Well, you're going ahead with the biography, aren't you?
I think you ought to.

NINA

(*Dryly.*)
For my soul, Doctor?
(*Listlessly.*)

139

I suppose I will. I don't know. I haven't much time. The duties of a wife –

(*Teasingly.*)

By the way, if it isn't too rude to inquire, aren't you getting yourself engaged to some fair lady or other?

DARRELL

(*Smiling – but emphatically.*)

Not on your life! Not until after I'm thirty-five, at least!

NINA

(*Sarcastically.*)

Then you don't believe in taking your own medicine? Why, Doctor! Think of how much good it would do you! –

(*Excitedly with a hectic sarcasm.*)

– if you had a nice girl to love – or was it learn to love? – and take care of – whose character you could shape and whose life you could guide and make what you pleased, in whose unselfish devotion you could find peace!

(*More and more bitterly sarcastic.*)

And you ought to have a baby, Doctor! You will never know what life is, you'll never be really happy until you've had a baby, Doctor – a fine, healthy baby!

(*She laughs a bitter, sneering laugh.*)

DARRELL

(*After a quick, keen glance, thinking.*)
Good! . . . she's going to tell . . .
(*Meekly.*)

I recognize my arguments. Was I really wrong on every point, Nina?

NINA

(*Harshly.*)

On every single point, Doctor!

DARRELL

(*Glancing at her keenly.*)

But how? You haven't given the baby end of it a chance yet, have you?

NINA

(*Bitterly.*)

Oh, haven't I?

(*Then bursts out with intense bitterness.*)

I'll have you know I'm not destined to bear babies, Doctor!

DARRELL

(*Startledly.*)

What's that? . . . why not? . . .

(*Again with a certain satisfaction.*)

Can she mean Sam? . . . that he . . .

(*Soothingly – but plainly disturbed.*)

Why don't you begin at the beginning and tell me all about it? I feel responsible.

NINA

(*Fiercely.*)

You are!

(*Then wearily.*)

And you're not. No one is. You didn't know. No one could know.

141

DARRELL

(*In same tone.*)

Know what?

(*Thinking with the same eagerness to believe something he hopes.*)
She must mean no one could know that Sam wasn't . . .
but I might have guessed it . . . from his general weakness
. . . poor unlucky devil! . . .
(*Then as she remains silent – urgingly.*)

Tell me. I want to help you, Nina.

NINA

(*Touched.*)

It's too late, Ned.

(*Then suddenly.*)

I've just thought – Sam said he happened to run into you.
That isn't so, is it? He went to see you and told you how
worried he was about me and asked you out to see me, didn't
he?

(*As Darrell nods.*)

Oh, I don't mind! It's even rather touching.

(*Then mockingly.*)

Well, since you're out here professionally, and my husband
wants me to consult you, I might as well give you the whole
case history!

(*Wearily.*)

I warn you it isn't pretty, Doctor! But then life doesn't
seem to be pretty, does it? And, after all, you aided and abetted
God the Father in making this mess. I hope it'll teach you
not to be so cocksure in future.

(*More and more bitterly.*)

142

I must say you proceeded very unscientifically, Doctor!

(Then suddenly starts her story in a dull monotonous tone recalling that of Evans' mother in the previous Act.)

When we went to visit Sam's mother I'd known for two months that I was going to have a baby.

DARRELL

(Startled – unable to hide a trace of disappointment.)

Oh, then you actually were?

(Thinking disappointedly and ashamed of himself for being disappointed.)
All wrong, what I thought . . . she was going to . . . then why didn't she? . .

NINA

(With a strange happy intensity.)

Oh, Ned, I loved it more than I've ever loved anything in my life – even Gordon! I loved it so it seemed at times that Gordon must be its real father, that Gordon must have come to me in a dream while I was lying asleep beside Sam! And I was happy! I almost loved Sam then! I felt he was a good husband!

DARRELL

(Instantly repelled – thinking with scornful jealousy.)
Ha! . . . the hero again! . . . comes to her bed! . . . puts horns on poor Sam! . . . becomes the father of his child! . . . I'll be damned if hers isn't the most idiotic obsession I ever . . .

NINA

(*Her voice suddenly becoming flat and lifeless.*)

And then Sam's mother told me I couldn't have my baby. You see, Doctor, Sam's great-grandfather was insane, and Sam's grandmother died in an asylum, and Sam's father had lost his mind for years before he died, and an aunt who is still alive is crazy. So of course I had to agree it would be wrong – and I had an operation.

DARRELL

(*Who has listened with amazed horror – profoundly shocked and stunned.*)

Good God! Are you crazy, Nina? I simply can't believe! It would be too hellish! Poor Sam, of all people!

(*Bewilderedly.*)

Nina! Are you absolutely sure?

NINA

(*Immediately defensive and mocking.*)

Absolutely, Doctor! Why? Do you think it's I who am crazy? Sam looks so healthy and sane, doesn't he? He fooled you completely, didn't he? You thought he'd be an ideal husband for me! And poor Sam's fooling himself too because he doesn't know anything about all this – so you can't blame him, Doctor!

DARRELL

(*Thinking in a real panic of horror – and a flood of protective affection for her.*)

God, this is too awful! . . . on top of all the rest! . . .

how did she ever stand it! . . . she'll lose her mind, too
. . . and it's my fault! . . .

> (*Getting up, comes to her and puts his hand on her
> shoulders, standing behind her – tenderly.*)

Nina! I'm so damn sorry! There's only one possible thing
to do now You'll have to make Sam give you a divorce.

NINA

(*Bitterly.*)

Yes? Then what do you suppose will be his finish? No,
I've enough guilt in my memory now, thank you! I've got
to stick to Sam!

> (*Then with a strange monotonous insistence.*)

I've promised Sam's mother I'd make him happy! He's
unhappy now because he thinks he isn't able to give me a
child. And I'm unhappy because I've lost my child. So I
must have another baby – somehow – don't you think, Doctor? – to make us both happy?

> (*She looks up at him pleadingly. For a moment they
> stare into each other's eyes – then both turn away
> in guilty confusion.*)

DARRELL

(*Bewilderedly thinking.*)

That look in her eyes . . . what does she want me to
think? . . . why does she talk so much about being happy?
. . . am I happy? . . . I don't know . what is happiness? . . .

(*Confusedly.*)

Nina, I don't know what to think.

NINA

(Thinking strangely.)
That look in his eyes . . . what did he mean? . . .
(With the same monotonous insistence.)

You must know what to think. I can't think it out myself any more. I need your advice – your *scientific* advice this time, if you please, Doctor. I've thought and thought about it. I've told myself it's what I ought to do. Sam's own mother urged me to do it. It's sensible and kind and just and good. I've told myself this a thousand times and yet I can't quite convince something in me that's afraid of something. I need the courage of someone who can stand outside and reason it out as if Sam and I were no more than guinea-pigs. You've got to help me, Doctor! You've got to show me what's the sane – the truly sane, you understand! – thing I must do for Sam's sake, and my own.

DARRELL

(Thinking confusedly.)

What do I have to do? . . . this was all my fault . . . I owe her something in return . . I owe Sam something . . . I owe them happiness! . . .
(Irritably.)
Damn it, there's a humming in my ears! . . . I've caught some fever . . . I swore to live coolly . . . let me see . . .
(In a cold, emotionless professional voice, his face like a mask of a doctor.)

A doctor must be in full possession of the facts, if he is to advise. What is it precisely that Sam's wife has thought so much of doing?

NINA

(In the same insistent tone.)

Of picking out a healthy male about whom she cared nothing and having a child by him that Sam would believe was
his child, whose life would give him confidence in his own
living, who would be for him a living proof that his wife
loved him.

(Confusedly, strangely and purposefully.)
This doctor is healthy. . . .

DARRELL

*(In his ultra-professional manner – like an automaton
of a doctor.)*

I see. But this needs a lot of thinking over. It isn't easy to
prescribe –

(Thinking.)
I have a friend who has a wife . . . I was envious at his
wedding . . . but what has that to do with it? . . . damn it,
my mind won't work! . . . it keeps running away to her
. . . it wants to mate with her mind . . . in the interest of
Science? . . . what damned rot I'm thinking! . . .

NINA

(Thinking as before.)
This doctor is nothing to me but a healthy male . . .
when he was Ned he once kissed me . . . but I cared nothing about him . . . so that's all right, isn't it, Sam's
Mother?

DARRELL

(Thinking.)
Let me see. . . . I am in the laboratory and they are
guinea-pigs . . . in fact, in the interest of Science, I can be,

for the purpose of this experiment, a healthy guinea-pig myself and still remain an observer . . . I observe my pulse is high, for example, and that's obviously because I am stricken with a recurrence of an old desire . . . desire is a natural male reaction to the beauty of the female . . . her husband is my friend. . . . I have always tried to help him . . .

(*Coldly.*)

I've been considering what Sam's wife told me and her reasoning is quite sound. The child can't be her husband's.

NINA

Then you agree with Sam's mother? She said: "Being happy is the nearest we can ever come to knowing what good is!"

DARRELL

I agree with her decidedly. Sam's wife should find a healthy father for Sam's child at once. It is her sane duty to her husband.

(*Worriedly thinking.*)

Have I ever been happy? . . . I have studied to cure the body's unhappiness . . . I have watched happy smiles form on the lips of the dying . . . I have experienced pleasure with a number of women I desired but never loved . . . I have known a bit of honour and a trifle of self-satisfaction . . . this talk of happiness seems to me extraneous . . .

NINA

(*Beginning to adopt a timid, diffident, guilty tone.*)

This will have to be hidden from Sam so he can never know! Oh, Doctor, Sam's wife is afraid!

STRANGE INTERLUDE

DARRELL

(Sharply professional.)

Nonsense! This is no time for timidity! Happiness hates the timid! So does Science! Certainly Sam's wife must conceal her action! To let Sam know would be insanely cruel of her — and stupid, for then no one could be the happier for her act!

(Anxiously thinking.)

Am I right to advise this? . . . yes, it is clearly the rational thing to do . . . but this advice betrays my friend! . . . no, it saves him! . . . it saves his wife . . . and if a third party should know a little happiness . . . is he any poorer, am I any the less his friend because I saved him? . . . no, my duty to him is plain . . . and my duty as an experimental searcher after truth . . . to observe these three guinea-pigs, of which I am one . . .

NINA

(Thinking determinedly.)

I must have my baby! . . .

(Timidly — gets from her chair and half turns toward him — pleadingly.)

You must give his wife courage, Doctor. You must free her from her feeling of guilt.

DARRELL

There can only be guilt when one deliberately neglects one's manifest duty to life. Anything else is rot! This woman's duty is to save her husband and herself by bearing a healthy child!

(Thinking guiltily and instinctively moving away from her.)

I am healthy . . . but he is my friend . . there is such a thing as honour! . . .

149

NINA

(*Determinedly.*)
I must take my happiness! . . .
(*Frightenedly – comes after him.*)

But she is ashamed. It's adultery. It's wrong.

DARRELL

(*Moving away again – with a cold sneering laugh of impatience.*)

Wrong! Would she rather see her husband wind up in an asylum? Would she rather face the prospect of going to pot herself, mentally, morally and physically, through year after year of devilling herself and him? Really, Madame, if you can't throw overboard all such irrelevant moral ideas, I'll have to give up this case here and now!

(*Thinking frightenedly.*)
Who is talking? . . . is he suggesting me? . . but you know very well I can't be the one, Doctor! . . . why not, you're healthy and it's a friendly act for all concerned. . . .

NINA

(*Thinking determinedly.*)
I must have my baby! . . .
(*Going further toward him – she can now touch him with her hand.*)

Please, Doctor, you must give her strength **to** do this right thing that seems to her so right and then so wrong!

(*She puts out her hand and takes one of his.*)

DARRELL

(*Thinking frightenedly.*)
Whose hand is this? . . . it burns me . . . I kissed her

150

once . . . her lips were cold . . . now they would burn with happiness for me! . . .

NINA

(Taking his other hand and slowly pulling him around to face her, although he does not look at her - pleadingly.)

Now she feels your strength. It gives her the courage to ask you, Doctor, to suggest the father. She has changed, Doctor, since she became Sam's wife. She can't bear the thought now of giving herself to any man she could neither desire nor respect. So each time her thoughts come to the man she must select they are afraid to go on! She needs your courage to choose!

DARRELL

(As if listening to himself.)

Sam is my friend . . . well, and isn't she your friend? . . . her two hands are so warm! . . . I must not even hint at my desire! . . .

(Judicially calm.)

Well, the man must be someone who is not unattractive to her physically, of course.

NINA

Ned always attracted her.

DARRELL

(Thinking frightenedly.)

What's that she said? . . . Ned? . . . attracts? . . ,

(In same tone.)

And the man should have a mind that can truly understand – a scientific mind superior to the moral scruples that cause so much human blundering and unhappiness.

NINA

She always thought Ned had a superior mind.

DARRELL

(*Thinking frightenedly.*)
Did she say Ned? . . . she thinks Ned . . ?
(*In same tone.*)

The man should like and admire her, he should be her good friend and want to help her, but he should not love her – although he might, without harm to anyone, desire her.

NINA

Ned does not love her – but he used to like her and, I think, desire her. Does he now, Doctor?

DARRELL

(*Thinking.*)
Does he? . . . who is he? . . . he is Ned! . . Ned is I!
. . . I desire her! . . . I desire happiness! . . .
(*Trembling now – gently.*)

But, Madame, I must confess the Ned you are speaking of is I, and I am Ned.

NINA

(*Gently.*)

And I am Nina, who wants her baby.

(*Then she reaches out and turns his head until his face faces hers, but he keeps his eyes down – she bends her head meekly and submissively – softly.*)

152

I should be so grateful, Ned.

> (*He starts, looks up at her wildly, makes a motion as though to take her in his arms, then remains fixed for a moment in that attitude, staring at her bowed head as she repeats submissively:*)

I should be so humbly grateful.

DARRELL

> (*Suddenly falling on his knees and taking her hand in both of his and kissing it humbly – with a sob.*)

Yes – yes, Nina – yes – for your happiness – in that spirit!

> (*Thinking – fiercely triumphant.*)

I shall be happy for a while! . . .

NINA

> (*Raising her head – thinking – proudly triumphant.*)

I shall be happy! . . . I shall make my husband happy! . . .

(*Curtain.*)

ACT FIVE

SCENE: *The sitting-room of a small house Evans has rented in a seashore suburb near New York. It is a bright morning in the following April.*

The room is a typical sitting-room of the quantity-production bungalow type. Windows on the left look out on a broad porch. A double doorway in rear leads into the hall. A door on right, to the dining-room. Nina has tried to take the curse of offensive, banal newness off the room with some of her own things from her old home, but the attempt has been half-hearted in the face of such overpowering commonness, and the result is a room as disorganized in character as was the Professor's study in the last Act.

The arrangement of the furniture follows the same pattern as in preceding scenes. There is a Morris chair and a round golden oak table at left of centre, an upholstered chair, covered with bright chintz at centre, a sofa covered with the same chintz at right.

Nina is sitting in the chair at centre. She has been trying to read a book, but has let this drop listlessly on her lap. A great change is noticeable in her face and bearing. She is again the pregnant woman of Act Three, but this time there is a triumphant strength about her expression, a ruthless self-confidence in her eyes. She has grown stouter, her face has filled out. One gets no impression of neurotic strain from her now, she seems nerveless and deeply calm.

NINA

(*As if listening for something within her – joyfully.*)
There! . . . that can't be my imagination . . . I felt it plainly . . . life . . . my baby . . . my only baby . . . the

154

other never really lived . . . this is the child of my love! . . .
I love Ned! . . . I've loved him ever since that first afternoon . . . when I went to him . . . so scientifically! . .

(*She laughs at herself.*)

Oh, what a goose I was! . . . then love came to me . . .
in his arms . . . happiness! . . . I hid it from him . . . I
saw he was frightened . . . his own joy frightened him . . .
I could feel him fighting with himself . . . during all those
afternoons . . . our wonderful afternoons of happiness! . . .
and I said nothing . . . I made myself be calculating . . . so
when he finally said . . . dreadfully disturbed . . . "Look
here, Nina, we've done all that is necessary, playing with
fire is dangerous" . . . I said, "You're quite right, Ned, of
all things I don't want to fall in love with you!" . . .

(*She laughs.*)

He didn't like that! . . . he looked angry . . . and afraid
. . . then for weeks he never even 'phoned . . . I waited
. . . it was prudent to wait . . . but every day I grew more
terrified . . . then just as my will was breaking, his broke
. . . he suddenly appeared again . . . but I held him to his
aloof doctor's pose and sent him away, proud of his will
power . . . and sick of himself with desire for me! . . .
every week since then he's been coming out here . . . as my
doctor . . . we've talked about our child wisely, dispas-
sionately . . . as if it were Sam's child . . . we've never
given in to our desire . . . and I've watched love grow in
him until I'm sure . . .

(*With sudden alarm.*)

But am I? . . . he's never once mentioned love . . . perhaps I've been a fool to play the part I've played . . . it
may have turned him against me . . .

(*Suddenly with calm confidence.*)

No . . he does . . . I feel it . . . it's only when I start
thinking I begin to doubt . . .

(*She settles back and stares dreamily before her – a
pause.*)

There . . . again . . . his child! . . . my child moving in
my life . . . my life moving in my child . . . the world is

whole and perfect . . . all things are each other's . . life
is . . . and the is is beyond reason . . . questions die in the
silence of this peace . . . I am living a dream within the
great dream of the tide . . . breathing in the tide I dream
and breathe back my dream into the tide . . . suspended in
the movement of the tide, I feel life move in me, suspended
in me . . . no whys matter . . . there is no why . . . I am a
mother . . . God is a Mother . . .

> (*She sighs happily, closing her eyes. A pause.*)
>
> (*Evans enters from the hallway in rear. He is
> dressed carefully but his clothes are old ones –
> shabby collegiate gentility – and he has forgotten
> to shave. His eyes look pitiably harried, his man-
> ner has become a distressingly obvious attempt to
> cover up a chronic state of nervous panic and
> guilty conscience. He stops inside the doorway
> and looks at her with a pitiable furtiveness, argu-
> ing with himself, trying to get up his courage.*)

EVANS

Tell her! . . . go on! . . . you made up your mind to,
didn't you? . . . don't quit now! . . . tell her you've decided . . . for her sake . . . to face the truth . . . that she
can't love you . . . she's tried . . . she's acted like a good
sport . . . but she's beginning to hate you . . . and you
can't blame her . . . she wanted children . . . and you
haven't been able . . .

> (*Protesting feebly.*)

But I don't know for certain . . . that that's my fault . .

> (*Then bitterly.*)

Aw, don't kid yourself, if she'd married someone else . . .
if Gordon had lived and married her . . . I'll bet in the first
month she'd . . . you'd better resign from the whole game
. . . with a gun! . . .

> (*He swallows hard as if he were choking back a sob –
> then savagely.*)

Stop whining! . . go on and wake her up! . . say

you're willing to give her a divorce so she can marry some
real guy who can give her what she ought to have! . .
> (*Then with sudden terror.*)

And if she says yes? . . . I couldn't bear it! . . . I'd die
without her! . . .
> (*Then with a sombre alien forcefulness.*)

All right . . . good riddance! . . . I'd have the guts to
bump off then, all right! . . . that'd set her free . . . come
on now! . . . ask her! . . .
> (*But his voice begins to tremble uncertainly again as
> he calls.*)

Nina!

NINA
> (*Opens her eyes and gazes calmly, indifferently at
> him.*)

Yes?

EVANS
> (*Immediately terrified and beaten – thinking.*)

I can't! . . . the way she looks at me! . . . she'd say
yes! . . .
> (*Stammering.*)

I hate to wake you up, but – it's about time for Ned to
come, isn't it?

NINA
> (*Calmly.*)

I wasn't asleep.
> (*Thinking as if she found it hard to concentrate on
> him, to realize his existence.*)

This man is my husband . . . it's hard to remember that
. . . people will say he's the father of my child. . . .
> (*With revulsion.*)

That's shameful! . . . and yet that's exactly what I
wanted! . . . wanted! . . . not now! . . . now I love Ned!
. . . I won't lose him! . . . Sam must give me a divorce

. . . I've sacrificed enough of my life . . . what has he given me? . . . not even a home . . . I had to sell my father's home to get money so we could move near his job . . . and then he lost his job! . . . now he's depending on Ned to help him get another! . . . my love! . . . how shameless! . . .
>   (*Then contritely.*)

Oh, I'm unjust . . . poor Sam doesn't know about Ned . . . and it was I who wanted to sell the place . . . I was lonely there . . . I wanted to be near Ned. . . .

EVANS

>   (*Thinking in agony.*)

What's she thinking? . . . probably lucky for me I don't know! . . .
>   (*Forcing a brisk air as he turns away from her.*)

I hope Ned brings that letter he promised me to the manager of the Globe Company. I'm keen to get on the job again.

NINA

>   (*With scornful pity.*)

Oh, I guess Ned will bring the letter. I asked him not to forget.

EVANS

I hope they'll have an opening right off. We can use the money.
>   (*Hanging his head.*)

I feel rotten, living on you when you've got so little.

NINA

>   (*Indifferently but with authority, like a governess to a small boy.*)

Now, now!

EVANS

(Relieved.)

Well, it's true.

(Then coming to her – humbly ingratiating.)

You've felt a lot better lately, haven't you, Nina?

NINA

(With a start – sharply.)

Why?

EVANS

You look ever so much better. You're getting fat.

(He forces a grin.)

NINA

(Curtly.)

Don't be absurd, please! As a matter of fact, I don't feel a bit better.

EVANS

(Thinking despondently.)

Lately, she jumps on me every chance she gets . . . as if everything I did disgusted her! . . .

(He strays over to the window and looks out listlessly.)

I thought we'd get some word from Charlie this morning saying if he was coming down or not. But I suppose he's still too broken up over his mother's death to write.

NINA

(Indifferently.)

He'll probably come without bothering to write.

(Vaguely – wonderingly.)

Charlie . . . dear old Charlie! . . . I've forgotten him, too. . . .

EVANS

I think that's Ned's car now. Yes. It's stopping. I'll go out and meet him.

(*He starts for the door in rear.*)

NINA

(*Sharply, before she can restrain the impulse.*)

Don't be such a fool!

EVANS

(*Stops – stammers confusedly.*)

What – what's the matter?

NINA

(*Controlling herself – but irritably.*)

Don't mind me. I'm nervous.

(*Thinking guiltily.*)

One minute I feel ashamed of him for making such a fool of himself over my lover . . . the next minute something hateful urges me to drive him into doing it! . . .

(*The maid has answered the ring and opened the outer door. Ned Darrell comes in from the rear. His face looks older. There is an expression of defensive bitterness and self-resentment about his mouth and eyes. This vanishes into one of desire and joy as he sees Nina.*)

DARRELL

(*He starts toward her impulsively.*)

Nina!

(*Then stops short as he sees Evans.*)

160

NINA

(*Forgetting Evans, gets to her feet as if to receive Darrell in her arms – with love.*)

Ned!

EVANS

(*Affectionately and gratefully.*)

Hallo, Ned!

(*He holds out his hand, which Darrell takes mechanically.*)

DARRELL

(*Trying to overcome his guilty embarrassment.*)

Hallo! Sam. Didn't see you.

(*Hurriedly reaching in his coat pocket.*)

Before I forget, here's that letter. I had a talk over the 'phone with Appleby yesterday. He's pretty sure there's an opening –

(*With a condescension he can't help.*)

– but you'll have to get your nose on the grindstone to make good with him.

EVANS

(*Flushing guiltily – forcing a confident tone.*)

You bet I will!

(*Then gratefully and humbly.*)

Gosh, Ned, I can't tell you how grateful I am!

DARRELL

(*Brusquely, to hide his embarrassment.*)

Oh, shut up! I'm only too glad.

NINA

(*Watching Evans with a contempt that is almost gloating – in a tone of curt dismissal.*)

You'd better go and shave, hadn't you, if you're going to town?

EVANS

(*Guiltily, passing his hand over his face – forcing a brisk, purposeful air.*)

Yes, of course. I forgot I hadn't. Excuse me, will you?

(*This to Darrell. Evans hurries out, rear.*)

DARRELL

(*As soon as he is out of earshot – turning on Nina accusingly.*)

How can you treat him that way? It makes me feel – like a swine!

NINA

(*Flushing guiltily – protestingly.*)

What way?

(*Then inconsequentially.*)

He's always forgetting to shave lately.

DARRELL

You know what I mean, Nina!

(*Turns away from her – thinking bitterly.*)

What a rotten liar I've become! . . . and he trusts me absolutely! . . .

162

NINA

(*Thinking frightenedly.*)
Why doesn't he take me in his arms? . . . oh, I feel he doesn't love me now! . . . he's so bitter! . . .
(*Trying to be matter-of-fact.*)

I'm sorry, Ned. I don't mean to be cross, but Sam does get on my nerves.

DARRELL

(*Thinking bitterly.*)
Sometimes I almost hate her! . . . if it wasn't for her I'd have kept my peace of mind . . . no good for anything lately, damn it! . . . but it's idiotic to feel guilty . . . if Sam only didn't trust me! . . .
(*Then impatiently.*)
Bosh! . . . sentimental nonsense! . . . end justifies means! . . . this will have a good end for Sam, I swear to that! . . . why doesn't she tell him she's pregnant? . . . what's she waiting for? . . .

NINA

(*Thinking passionately, looking at him.*)
Oh, my lover, why don't you kiss me? . . .
(*Imploringly.*)

Ned! Don't be cross with me, please!

DARRELL

(*Fighting to control himself – coldly.*)

I'm not cross, Nina. Only you must admit these triangular scenes are, to say the least, humiliating.

(*Resentfully.*)

I won't come out here again!

NINA

(*With a cry of pain.*)

Ned!

DARRELL

(*Thinking exultingly at first.*)

She loves me! . . . she's forgotten Gordon! . . . I'm happy! . . . do I love her? . . . no! . . . I won't! . . . I can't! . . . think what it would mean to Sam! . . . to my career! . . . be objective about it! . . . you guinea-pig! . . . I'm her doctor . . . and Sam's . . . I prescribed child for them . . . that's all there is to it! . . .

NINA

(*Torn between hope and fear.*)

What is he thinking? . . . he's fighting his love . . . oh, my lover! . . .

(*Again with longing.*)

Ned!

DARRELL

(*Putting on his best professional air, going to her.*)

How do you feel to-day? You look as if you might have a little fever.

(*He takes her hand as if to feel her pulse.*)
(*Her hand closes over his. She looks up into his face. He keeps his turned away.*)

NINA

(*Straining up toward him – with intense longing – thinking.*)

I love you! . . . take me! . . . what do I care for anything in the world but you! . . . let Sam die! . . .

DARRELL

(*Fighting himself – thinking.*)
Christ! . . . touch of her skin! . . . her nakedness! . . .
those afternoons in her arms! happiness! . . . what do I care
for anything else! . . . to hell with Sam! . . .

NINA

(*Breaking out passionately.*)

Ned! I love you! I can't hide it any more! I won't! I
love you, Ned!

DARRELL

(*Suddenly taking her in his arms and kissing her frantically.*)

Nina! Beautiful!

NINA

(*Triumphantly – between kisses.*)

You love me, don't you? Say you do, Ned!

DARRELL

(*Passionately.*)

Yes! Yes!

NINA

(*With a cry of triumph.*)

Thank God! At last you've told me! You've confessed it
to yourself! Oh, Ned, you've made me so happy!

> (*There is a ring from the front-door bell. Darrell
> hears it. It acts like an electric shock on him. He
> tears himself away from her. Instinctively she
> gets up too and moves to the lounge at right.*)

DARRELL

(*Stupidly.*)

Someone – at the door.

> (*He sinks down in the chair by the table at left.*)
> (*Thinking torturedly.*)
> I said I loved her! . . . she won! . . . she used my desire!
> . . . but I don't love her! . . . I won't! . . . she can't own
> my life! . . .
> (*Violently – almost shouts at her.*)

I don't, Nina! I tell you I don't!

NINA

> (*The maid has just gone to the front door.*)

Sshh!

> (*Then in a triumphant whisper.*)

You do, Ned! You do!

DARRELL

> (*With dogged stupidity.*)

I don't!

> (*The front door has been opened. Marsden appears in
> the rear, walks slowly and woodenly like a man
> in a trance into the room. He is dressed imma-
> culately in deep mourning. His face is pale,
> drawn, haggard with loneliness and grief. His
> eyes have a dazed look as if he were still too
> stunned to comprehend clearly what has hap-
> pened to him. He does not seem conscious of
> Darrell's presence at first. His shoulders are
> bowed, his whole figure droops.*)

NINA

(Thinking – in a strange superstitious panic.)
Black . . . in the midst of happiness . . . black comes
. . . again . . . death . . . my father . . . comes between
me and happiness! . . .
(Then recovering herself, scornfully.)
You silly coward! . . . it's only Charlie! . . .
(Then furious with resentment.)
The old fool! . . . what does he mean coming in on us
without warning? . . .

MARSDEN

(Forcing a pitiful smile to his lips.)

Hallo, Nina! I know it's an imposition – but – I've been
in such a terrible state since Mother –

*(He falters, his face becomes distorted into an ugly
mask of grief, his eyes water.)*

NINA

*(Immediately sympathetic, gets up and goes to him
impulsively.)*

There's no question of imposition, Charlie. We were
expecting you.

*(She has come to him and put her arms around him.
He gives way and sobs, his head against her
shoulder.)*

MARSDEN

(Brokenly.)

You don't know, Nina – how terrible – it's terrible! –

NINA

(*Leading him to the chair at centre, soothingly.*)

I know, Charlie.

(*Thinking with helpless annoyance.*)
Oh, dear, what can I say? . . . his mother hated me . . .
I'm not glad she's dead . . . but neither am I sorry . . .
(*With a trace of contempt.*)
Poor Charlie! . . . he was so tied to her apron strings . . .
(*Then kindly but condescendingly, comforting him.*)

Poor old Charlie!

MARSDEN

(*The words and the tone shock his pride to life. He
raises his head and half pushes her away —
resentfully, thinking.*)
Poor old Charlie! . . . damn it, what am I to her? . . .
her old dog who's lost his mother? . . . Mother hated her
. . no, poor dear Mother was so sweet, she never hated
anyone . . . she simply disapproved . . .
(*Coldly.*)

I'm all right, Nina. Quite all right now, thank you. I
apologize for making a scene.

DARRELL

(*Has got up from his chair – with relief – thinking.*)
Thank God for Marsden . . . I feel sane again . . .
(*He comes to Marsden – cordially.*)

How are you, Marsden?

(*Then offering conventional consolation, pats Marsden's shoulder.*)

I'm sorry, Marsden.

STRANGE INTERLUDE

MARSDEN

(*Startled, looks up at him in amazement.*)

Darrell!

(*Then with instant hostility.*)

There's nothing to be sorry about that I can discover!

(*Then as they both look at him in surprise he realizes what he has said – stammeringly.*)

I mean – sorry – is hardly the right word – hardly – is it?

NINA

(*Worriedly.*)

Sit down, Charlie. You look so tired.

(*He slumps down in the chair at centre mechanically. Nina and Darrell return to their chairs. Nina looks across him at Darrell – triumphantly – thinking.*)

You do love me, Ned! . . .

DARRELL

(*Thinking – answering her look – defiantly.*)

I don't love you! . . .

MARSDEN

(*Stares intensely before him. Thinking suspiciously-morbidly agitated.*)

Darrell! . . . and Nina! . . . there's something in this room! . . . something disgusting! . . . like a brutal, hairy hand, raw and red, at my throat! . . . stench of human life! . . . heavy and rank! . . . outside it's April . . . green buds on the slim trees . . . the sadness of spring . . . my loss at peace in Nature . . . her sorrow of birth consoling my sorrow of death . . . something human and unnatural in this room! . . . love and hate and passion and possession!

. . . cruelly indifferent to my loss! . . . mocking my loneliness! . . . no longer any love for me in any room! . . . lust in this room! . . . lust with a loathsome jeer taunting my sensitive timidities! . . . my purity! . . . purity? . . . ha! yes, if you say prurient purity! . . . lust ogling me for a dollar with oily shoe-button Italian eyes! . . .

> (*In terror.*)

What thoughts! . . . what a low scoundrel you are! . . . and your mother dead only two weeks! . . . I hate Nina! . . . that Darrell in this room! . . . I feel their desires! . . . where is Sam? . . . I'll tell him! . . . no, he wouldn't believe . . . he's such a trusting fool . . . I must punish her some other way . . .

> (*Remorsefully.*)

What? . . . punish Nina? . . . my little Nina? . . . why, I want her to be happy! . . . even with Darrell? . . . it's all so confused! . . . I must stop thinking! . . . I must talk! . . . forget! . . . say something! . . . forget everything! . . .

> (*He suddenly bursts into a flood of garrulity.*)

Mother asked for you, Nina – three days before the end. She said, "Where is Nina Leeds now, Charlie? When is she going to marry Gordon Shaw?" Her mind was wandering, poor woman! You remember how fond she always was of Gordon? She used to love to watch the football games when he was playing. He was so handsome and graceful, she always thought. She always loved a strong, healthy body. She took such strict care of her own, she walked miles every day, she loved bathing and boating in the summer even after she was sixty, she was never sick a day in her life until –

> (*He turns on Darrell – coldly.*)

You were right, Doctor Darrell. It was cancer.

> (*Then angrily.*)

But the doctor you sent me to, and the other he called in, could do nothing for her – absolutely nothing! I might just

as well have imported some witch doctors from the Solomon
Islands! They at least would have diverted her in her last
hours with their singing and dancing, but your specialists
were a total loss!

(*Suddenly with an insulting, ugly sneer, raising his
voice.*)

I think you doctors are a pack of God-damned ignorant
liars and hypocrites!

NINA

(*Sharply.*)

Charlie!

MARSDEN

(*Coming to himself – with a groan – shamefacedly.*)

Don't mind me. I'm not myself, Nina. I've been through
hell!

(*He seems about to sob – then abruptly springs to his
feet, wildly.*)

It's this room! I can't stand this room! There's something
repulsive about it!

NINA

(*Soothingly.*)

I know it's ugly, Charlie. I haven't had a chance to fix it
up yet. We've been too broke.

MARSDEN

(*Confusedly.*)

Oh, it's all right. I'm ugly, too! Where's Sam?

171

NINA

(*Eagerly.*)

Right upstairs. Go on up. He'll be delighted to see you.

MARSDEN

(*Vaguely.*)

Very well.

(*He goes to the door, then stops mournfully.*)

But from what I saw on that visit to his home, he doesn't love his mother much. I don't think he'll understand, Nina. He never writes to her, does he?

NINA

(*Uneasily.*)

No – I don't know.

MARSDEN

She seemed lonely. He'll be sorry for it some day after she –

(*He gulps.*)

Well –

(*He goes.*)

NINA

(*In a sudden pause – thinking.*)

Sam's mother! . . . "Make my boy, Sammy, happy!"
. . . I promised . . . oh, why did Charlie have to remember her? . . .

(*Then resolutely.*)

I can't remember her now! . . . I won't! . . . I've got to be happy! . . .

172

DARRELL

(*Uneasily trying to force a casual conversation.*)

Poor Marsden is completely knocked off balance, isn't he?

(*A pause.*)

My mother died when I was away at school. I hadn't seen her for some time, so her death was never very real to me; but in Marsden's case –

NINA

(*With a possessive smile of tolerance.*)

Never mind Charlie, Ned. What do I care about Charlie? I love you! And you love me!

DARRELL

(*Apprehensively, forcing a tone of annoyed rebuke.*)

But I don't! And you don't! You're simply letting your romantic imagination run away with you –

(*Showing his jealous resentment in spite of himself.*)

– as you did once before with Gordon Shaw!

NINA

(*Thinking.*)

He is jealous of Gordon! . . . how wonderful that is! . . .

(*With provoking calm.*)

I loved Gordon.

DARRELL

(*Irritably ignoring this as if he didn't want to hear it.*)

Romantic imagination! It has ruined more lives than all

173

the diseases! Other diseases, I should say! It's a form of insanity!

> (*He gets up forcefully and begins to pace about the room.*)
> (*Thinking uneasily.*)
> Mustn't look at her . . . find an excuse and get away . . . and this time never come back! . . .
> (*Avoiding looking at her, trying to argue reasonably – coldly.*)

You're acting foolishly, Nina – and very unfairly. The agreement we made has no more to do with love than a contract for building a house. In fact, you know we agreed it was essential that love mustn't enter into it. And it hasn't, in spite of what you say.

> (*A pause. He walks about. She watches him.*)
> (*Thinking.*)
> She's got to come back to earth! . . . I've got to break with her! . . . bad enough now! . . . but to go on with it! . . . what a mess it'd make of all our lives! . . .

NINA

> (*Thinking tenderly.*)
> Let his pride put all the blame on me! . . . I'll accept it gladly! . . .

DARRELL

(*Irritably.*)

Of course, I realize I've been to blame, too. I haven't been able to be as impersonal as I thought I could be. The trouble is there's been a dangerous physical attraction. Since I first met you, I've always desired you physically. I admit that now.

NINA

(*Smiling tenderly – thinking.*)
Oh, he admits that, does he? . . . poor darling! . . .
(*Enticingly.*)

And you still do desire me, don't you, Ned?

DARRELL

(*Keeping his back turned to her – roughly.*)

No! That part of it is finished!

(*Nina laughs softly, possessively. He whirls around
to face her – angrily.*)

Look here! You're going to have the child you wanted,
aren't you?

NINA

(*Implacably.*)

My child wants its father!

DARRELL

(*Coming a little toward her – desperately.*)

But you're crazy! You're forgetting Sam! It may be stupid,
but I've got a guilty conscience! I'm beginning to think
we've wronged the very one we were trying to help!

NINA

You were trying to help me, too, Ned!

175

DARRELL

(*Stammering.*)

Well – all right – let's say that part of it was all right then. But it's got to stop! It can't go on!

NINA

(*Implacably.*)

Only your love can make me happy now! Sam must give me a divorce so I can marry you.

DARRELL

(*Thinking suspiciously.*)
Look out! . . . there it is! . . . marry! . . . own me! . . . ruin my career! . . .
(*Scornfully.*)

Marry? Do you think I'm a fool? Get that out of your head quick! I wouldn't marry anyone – no matter what!

(*As she continues to look at him with unmoved determination – pleadingly.*)

Be sensible, for God's sake! We're absolutely unsuited to each other! I don't admire your character! I don't respect you! I know too much about your past!

(*Then indignantly.*)

And how about Sam? Divorce him? Have you forgotten all his mother told you? Do you mean to say you'd deliberately – ? And you expect me to – ? What do you think I am?

NINA

(*Inflexibly.*)

You're my lover! Nothing else matters. Yes, I remember what Sam's mother said. She said, "being happy is the nearest we can come to knowing what good is." And I'm going to be happy! I've lost everything in life so far because I didn't have the courage to take it – and I've hurt everyone around me. There's no use trying to think of others. One human being can't think of another. It's impossible.

(*Gently and caressingly.*)

But this time I'm going to think of my own happiness – and that means you – and our child! That's quite enough for one human being to think of, dear, isn't it?

> (*She reaches out and takes his hand. A pause. With her other hand she gently pulls him around until he is forced to look into her eyes.*)

DARRELL

(*Thinking fascinatedly.*)
I see my happiness in her eyes . . . the touch of her soft skin! . . . those afternoons! . . . God, I was happy! . . .
> (*In a strange dazed voice – as if it were forced out of him by an impulse stronger than his will.*)

Yes, Nina.

NINA

(*In a determined voice.*)

I've given Sam enough of my life! And it hasn't made him happy, not the least bit! So what's the good? And how can we really know that his thinking our child was his would do him any good? We can't! It's all guesswork. The only thing sure is that we love each other.

DARRELL

(*Dazedly.*)
Yes.

STRANGE INTERLUDE

(A noise from the hall and Evans comes in from the rear. He sees their two hands together, but mistakes their meaning.)

EVANS

(Genially – with a forced self-confident air.)

Well, Doc, how's the patient? I think she's much better, don't you? – although she won't admit it.

DARRELL

(At the first sound of Evans' voice, pulls his hand from Nina's as if it were a hot coal – avoiding Evans' eyes, moving away from her jerkily and self-consciously.)

Yes. Much better.

EVANS

Good!

(He pats Nina on the back. She shrinks away. His confidence vanishes in a flash.)
(Thinking miserably.)
Why does she shrink away . . . if I even touch her? . . .

NINA

(Matter-of-factly.)

I must see how lunch is coming on. You'll stay, of course, Ned?

DARRELL

(Struggling – shakenly.)

No, I think I'd better –

(Thinking desperately.)
Got to go! . . . can't go! . . . got to go! . . .

178

EVANS

Oh, come on, old man!

NINA

(*Thinking.*)
He must stay . . . and after lunch we'll tell Sam. . . .
(*With certainty.*)

He'll stay.

(*Meaningly.*)

And we want to have a long talk with you after lunch, Sam
– don't we, Ned?

(*Darrell does not answer. She goes out, right.*)

EVANS

(*Vaguely making talk.*)

I got Charlie to lie down. He's all in, poor guy.

(*Then trying to face Darrell, who keeps looking away
from him.*)

What did Nina mean, you want a long talk with me? Or is
it a secret, Ned?

DARRELL

(*Controlling an impulse toward hysterical laughter.*)

A secret? Yes, you bet it's a secret!

(*He flings himself in the chair at left, keeping his face
averted.*)

(*His thoughts bitter and desperate like a cornered
fugitive's.*)

This is horrible! . . . Sam thinks I'm finest fellow in
world . . . and I do this to him! . . . as if he hadn't
enough! . . . born under a curse! . . . I finish him! . . . a

doctor! . . . God damn it! . . . I can see his end! . . . never forgive myself! . . . never forget! . . . break me! . . . ruin my career! . . .

> (*More desperately.*)

Got to stop this! . . . while there's time! . . . she said . . . after lunch, talk . . . she meant, tell him . . . that means kill him . . . then she'll marry me! . . .

> (*Beginning to be angry.*)

By God, I won't! . . . she'll find out! . . . smiling! . . . got me where she wants me! . . . then be as cruel to me as she is to him! . . . love me? . . . liar! . . . still loves Gordon! . . . her body is a trap! . . . I'm caught in it! . . . she touches my hand, her eyes get in mine, I lose my will! . . .

> (*Furiously.*)

By God, she can't make a fool of me that way! . . . I'll go away to some place! . . . go to Europe! . . . study! . . . forget her in work! . . . keep hidden until boat sails so she can't reach me! . . .

> (*He is in a state of strange elation by this time.*)

Go now! . . . no! . . . got to spike her guns with Sam! . . . by God, I see! . . . tell him about baby! . . . that'll stop her! . . . when she knows I've told him that, she'll see it's hopeless! . . . she'll stick to him! . . . poor Nina! . . . I'm sorry! . . . she does love me! . . . hell! . . . she'll forget! . . . she'll have her child! . . . she'll be happy! . . . and Sam'll be happy! . . .

> (*He suddenly turns to Evans, who has been staring at him, puzzledly – in a whisper.*)

Look here, Sam. I can't stay to lunch. I haven't time, I've got a million things to do. I'm sailing for Europe in a few days.

EVANS

> (*Surprised.*)

You're sailing?

DARRELL

(*Very hurriedly.*)

Yes – going to study over there for a year or so. I haven't told anyone. I came out to-day to say good-bye. You won't be able to reach me again. I'll be out of town visiting.

(*Then elatedly.*)

And now for your secret! It ought to make you very happy, Sam. I know how much you've wished for it, so I'm going to tell you, although Nina'll be furious with me. She was saving it to surprise you with at her own proper time –

(*Still more elatedly.*)

– but I'm selfish enough to want to see you happy before I go!

EVANS

(*Not daring to believe what he hopes – stammering.*)

What – what is it, Ned?

DARRELL

(*Clapping him on the back – with strange joviality.*)

You're going to be a father, old scout, that's the secret!

(*Then as Evans just stares at him dumbly in a blissful satisfaction, he rattles on.*)

And now I've got to run. See you again in a year or so. I've said good-bye to Nina. Good-bye, Sam.

(*He takes his hand and clasps it.*)

Good luck! Buckle down to work now! You've got the stuff in you! When I get back I'll expect to hear you're on

181

the highroad to success! And tell Nina I'll expect to find you both happy in your child — both of you, tell her! — happy in your child! Tell her that, Sam!

> (*He turns and goes to the door.*)
> (*Thinking as he goes.*)
> That does it! . . . honourably! . . . I'm free! . . .
> > (*He goes out — then through the front door — a moment later his motor is heard starting — dies away.*)

EVANS

> (*Stares after him dumbly in the same state of happy stupefaction — mumbles.*)

Thank you — Ned!

> (*Thinking disjointedly.*)
> Why did I doubt myself? . . . now she loves me . . . she's loved me right along . . . I've been a fool . . .
> > (*He suddenly falls on his knees.*)
> O God, I thank you!
> > (*Nina comes in from the kitchen. She stops in amazement when she sees him on his knees. He jumps to his feet and takes her in his arms with confident happiness and kisses her.*)

Oh, Nina, I love you so! And now I know you love me! I'll never be afraid of anything again!

NINA

> (*Bewildered and terror-stricken, trying feebly to push him away — thinking.*)
> Has he . . . has he gone crazy? . . .
> (*Weakly.*)

Sam! What's come over you, Sam?

EVANS

(*Tenderly.*)

Ned told me – the secret – and I'm so happy, dear!
(*He kisses her again.*)

NINA

(*Stammering.*)

Ned told you – what?

EVANS

(*Tenderly.*)

That we're going to have a child, dear. You mustn't be sore at him. Why did you want to keep it a secret from me? Didn't you know how happy it would make me, Nina?

NINA

He told you we – we – you, the father – ?
(*Then suddenly breaking from him – wildly.*)

Ned! Where is Ned?

EVANS

He left a moment ago.

NINA

(*Stupidly.*)

Left? Call him back. Lunch is ready.

EVANS

He's gone. He couldn't stay. He's got so much to do getting ready to sail.

NINA

Sail?

EVANS

Didn't he tell you he was sailing for Europe? He's going over for a year or so to study.

NINA

A year or so!

(*Wildly.*)

I've got to call him up! No, I'll go in and see him right now!

(*She takes a wavering step toward the door.*)
(*Thinking in anguish.*)

Go! . . . go to him! . . . find him! . . . my lover! . . .

EVANS

He won't be there, I'm afraid. He said we couldn't reach him, that he'd be visiting friends out of town until he sailed.

(*Solicitously.*)

Why, do you have to see him about something important, Nina? Perhaps I could locate –

NINA

(*Stammering and swaying.*)

No.

(*She stifles an hysterical laugh.*)

No, nothing – nothing important – nothing is important – ha – !

(*She stifles another laugh – then on the verge of fainting, weakly.*)

Sam! Help me –

184

EVANS

(Rushes to her, supports her to sofa at right.)

Poor darling! Lie down and rest.

(She remains in a sitting position, staring blankly before her. He chafes her wrists.)

Poor darling!

(Thinking jubilantly.)

Her condition . . this weakness comes from her condition! . ,

NINA

(Thinking in anguish.)

Ned doesn't love me! . . . he's gone! . . . gone for ever! . . . like Gordon! . . . no, not like Gordon! . . . like a sneak, a coward! . . . a liar! . . . oh, I hate him! . . . O Mother God, please let me hate him! . . . he must have been planning this! . . . he must have known it to-day when he said he loved me! . . .

(Thinking frenziedly.)

I won't bear it! . . . he thinks he has palmed me off on Sam for ever! . . . and his child! . . . he can't! . . . I'll tell Sam he was lying! . . . I'll make Sam hate him! . . . I'll make Sam kill him! . . . I'll promise to love Sam if he kills him! . . .

(Suddenly turns to Evans – savagely.)

He lied to you!

EVANS

(Letting her wrists drop – appalled – stammers.)

You mean – Ned lied about – ?

NINA

(In same tone.)

Ned lied to you!

EVANS

(Stammers.)

You're not – going to have a child –

NINA

(Savagely.)

Oh, yes! Oh, yes, I am! Nothing can keep me from that! But you're – you're – I mean, you . . .

(Thinking in anguish.)
I can't say that to him! . . . I can't tell him without Ned to help me! . . . I can't! . . . look at his face! . . . oh, poor Sammy! . . . poor little boy! . . . poor little boy! . .

(She takes his head and presses it to her breast and begins to weep.)
(Weeping.)

I mean, you weren't to know about it, Sammy.

EVANS

(Immediately on the crest again – tenderly.)

Why? Don't you want me to be happy, Nina?

NINA

Yes – yes, I do, Sammy.

(Thinking strangely.)
Little boy! . . . little boy! . . . one gives birth to little boys! . . . one doesn't drive them mad and kill them! . . .

EVANS

(Thinking.)
She's never called me Sammy before . . . someone used to . . . oh, yes, Mother. . . .
(Tenderly and boyishly.)

And I'm going to make you happy from now on, Nina. I tell you, the moment Ned told me, something happened to me! I can't explain it, but – I'll make good now, Nina! I know I've said that before, but I was only boasting. I was only trying to make myself think so. But now I say it knowing I can do it!

(Softly.)

It's because we're going to have a child, Nina. I knew that you'd never really come to love me without that. That's what I was down on my knees for when you came in. I was thanking God – for our baby!

NINA

(Tremblingly.)

Sammy! Poor boy!

EVANS

Ned said when he came back he'd expect to find us both happy – in our baby. He said to tell you that. You will be happy now, won't you, Nina?

NINA

(Brokenly and exhaustedly.)

I'll try to make you happy, Sammy.

> *(He kisses her, then hides his head on her breast. She stares out over his head. She seems to grow older.)*
>
> *(Thinking as if she were repeating the words of some inner voice of life.)*

Not Ned's child! . . . not Sam's child! . . . mine! . . . there! . . . again! . . . I feel my child live . . . moving in my life . . . my life moving in my child . . . breathing in

the tide I dream and breathe my dream back into the tide
. . . God is a Mother! . . .

(Then with sudden anguish.)

Oh, afternoons . . . dear wonderful afternoons of love
with you, my lover! . . . you are lost . . . gone from me for
ever! . . .

(Curtain.)

SECOND PART

SECOND PART

ACT SIX

SCENE: *The same — an evening a little over a year later. The room has undergone a significant change. There is a comfortable, homy atmosphere as though now it definitely belonged to the type of person it was built for. It has a proud air of modest prosperity.*

It is soon after dinner — about eight o'clock. Evans is sitting by the table at left, glancing through a newspaper at headlines and reading an article here and there. Nina is in the chair at centre, knitting a tiny sweater. Marsden is sitting on the sofa at right, holding a book which he pretends to be looking through, but glancing wonderingly at Evans and Nina.

There is a startling change in Evans. He is stouter, the haggard look of worry and self-conscious inferiority has gone from his face, it is full and healthy and satisfied. There is also, what is more remarkable, a decided look of solidity about him, of a determination moving toward ends it is confident it can achieve. He has matured, found his place in the world.

The change in Nina is also perceptible. She looks noticeably older, the traces of former suffering are marked on her face, but there is also an expression of present contentment and calm.

Marsden has aged greatly. His hair is grey, his expression one of a deep grief that is dying out into a resignation resentful of itself. He is dressed immaculately in dark tweed.

NINA

(*Thinking.*)
i wonder if there's a draught in the baby's room? . . . maybe I'd better close the window? . . . oh, I guess it's all

191

right . . . he needs lots of fresh air . . . little Gordon . . .
he does remind me of Gordon . . . something in his eyes
. . . my romantic imagination? . . . Ned said that . . . why
hasn't Ned ever written? . . . it's better he hasn't . . . how
he made me suffer! . . . but I forgive him . . . he gave me
my baby . . . the baby certainly doesn't look like him . . .
every one says he looks like Sam . . . how absurd! . . . but
Sam makes a wonderful father . . . he's become a new man
in the past year . . . and I've helped him . . . he asks me
about everything . . . I have a genuine respect for him now
. . . I can give myself without repulsion . . . I am making
him happy . . . I've written his mother I'm making him
happy . . . I was proud to be able to write her that . . . how
queerly things work out! . . . all for the best . . . and I
don't feel wicked . . . I feel good . . .

(*She smiles strangely.*)

MARSDEN

(*Thinking.*)

What a change! . . . the last time I was here the air was
poisoned . . . Darrell . . . I was sure he was her lover . . .
but I was in a morbid state . . . why did Darrell run away?
. . Nina could have got Sam to divorce her if she really
loved Darrell . . . then it's evident she couldn't have loved
him . . . and she was going to have Sam's baby . . . Darrell's love must have seemed like treachery . . . so she sent
him away . . . that must be it! . . .

(*With satisfaction.*)

Yes, I've got it straight now. . . .

(*With contemptuous pity.*)

Poor Darrell . . . I have no use for him, but I did pity
him when I ran across him in Munich . . . he was going the
pace . . . looked desperate. . . .

(*Then gloomily.*)

My running away was about as successful as his . . . as
if one could leave one's memory behind! . . . I couldn't

forget Mother . . . she haunted me through every city of
Europe . . .

    (*Then irritatedly.*)

I must get back to work! . . . not a line written in over a
year! . . . my public will be forgetting me! . . . a plot came
to me yesterday . . . my mind is coming around again . . .
I am beginning to forget, thank God! . . .

    (*Then remorsefully.*)

No, I don't want to forget you, Mother! . . . but let me
remember . . . without pain! . . .

EVANS

(*Turning over a page of his paper.*)

There's going to be the biggest boom before long this
country has ever known, or I miss my guess, Nina.

NINA

(*With great seriousness.*)

Do you think so, Sammy?

EVANS

(*Decidedly.*)

I'm dead sure of it.

NINA

(*With a maternal pride and amusement.*)

Dear Sam . . . I can't quite believe in this self-confident
business man yet . . . but I have to admit he's proved it
. . . he asked for more money and they gave it without
question . . . they're anxious to keep him . . . they ought
to be . . . how he's slaved! . . for me and my baby! . . .

(Has been looking at Marsden surreptitiously over his paper.)

Charlie's mother must have hoarded up a half-million . . . he'll let it rot in Government bonds . . . wonder what he'd say if I proposed that he back me? . . . he's always taken a friendly interest . . . well, it's worth a bet, anyway . . . he'd be an easy partner to handle . . .

MARSDEN

(Staring at Evans wonderingly.)

What a changed Sam! . . . I preferred him the old way . . . futile, but he had a sensitive quality . . . now he's hardened . . . a little success . . . oh, he'll succeed all right . . . his kind are inheriting the earth . . . hogging it, cramming it down their tasteless gullets! . . . and he's happy! . . . actually happy! . . . he has Nina . . . a beautiful baby . . . a comfortable home . . . no sorrow, no tragic memories . . . and I have nothing . . . but utter loneliness! . . .

(With grieving self-pity.)

If only Mother had lived! . . . how horribly I miss her! . . . my lonely home . . . who will keep house for me now? . . . it has got to be done sympathetically or I shan't be able to work . . . I must write to Jane . . . she'll probably be only too glad . . .

(Turning to Nina.)

I think I'll write to my sister in California and ask her to come and live with me. She's alone now that her youngest daughter is married, and she has very little money. And my hands are tied as far as sharing the estate with her is concerned. According to Mother's will, I'm cut off too if I give her a penny. Mother never got over her bitter feeling about Jane's marriage. In a way, she was right. Jane's husband wasn't much – no family or position or ability – and I doubt if she was ever happy with him.

> (*Sarcastically.*)

It was one of those love matches!

NINA

> (*Smiling – teasingly.*)

There's no danger of your ever making a love match, is there, Charlie?

MARSDEN

> (*Wincing – thinking.*)
> She can't believe any woman could possibly love me! . . .
> (*Caustically.*)

I trust I'll never make that kind of a fool of myself, Nina!

NINA

> (*Teasingly.*)

Pooh! Aren't you the superior bachelor! I don't see anything to be so proud of! You're simply shirking, Charlie!

MARSDEN

> (*Wincing, but forcing a teasing air.*)

You were my only true love, Nina. I made a vow of perpetual bachelorhood when you threw me over in Sam's favour!

EVANS

> (*Has listened to this last – jokingly.*)

Hallo! What's this? I never knew you were my hated rival, Charlie!

MARSDEN

(*Dryly.*)

Oh – didn't you really?

(*But Evans has turned back to his paper.*)
(*Thinking savagely.*)
That fool, too! . . . he jokes about it! . . . as if I were the last one in the world he could imagine . . .

NINA

(*Teasingly.*)

Well, if I'm responsible, Charlie, I feel I ought to do something about it. I'll pick out a wife for you – guaranteed to suit! She must be at least ten years older than you, large and matronly and placid, and a wonderful cook and housekeeper –

MARSDEN

(*Sharply.*)

Don't be stupid!

(*Thinking angrily.*)
She picks someone beyond the age! . . . she never imagines sex could enter into it! . . .

NINA

(*Placatingly – seeing he is really angry.*)

Why, I was only picking out a type I thought would be good for you, Charlie – and for your work.

MARSDEN

(*Sneeringly – with a meaning emphasis.*)

You didn't mention chaste. I couldn't respect a woman who hadn't respected herself!

196

NINA

(*Thinking – stung.*)
He's thinking of those men in the hospital . . . what a
fool I was ever to tell him! . . .
(*Cuttingly.*)

Oh, so you think you deserve an innocent virgin!

MARSDEN

(*Coldly – controlling his anger.*)

Let's drop me, if you please.
(*With a look at her that is challenging and malicious.*)

Did I tell you I ran into Doctor Darrell in Munich?

NINA

(*Startled – thinking frightenedly and confusedly.*)
Ned! . . . he saw Ned! . . . why hasn't he told me before?
. . . why did he look at me like that? . . . does he suspect? . . .
(*Trying to be calm, but stammering.*)

You saw – Ned?

MARSDEN

(*With savage satisfaction.*)
That struck home! . . . look at her! . . . guilty! . . . then
I was right that day! . . .
(*Casually.*)

Yes, I chanced to run into him.

NINA

(*More calmly now.*)

Why on earth didn't you tell us before, Charlie?

197

MARSDEN

(Coolly.)

Why? Is it such important news? You knew he was there, didn't you? I supposed he'd written you.

EVANS

(Looking up from his paper – affectionately.)

How was the old scout?

MARSDEN

(Maliciously.)

He seemed in fine feather – said he was having a gay time. When I saw him he was with a startling-looking female – quite beautiful, if you like that type. I gathered they were living together.

NINA

(Cannot restrain herself – breaks out.)

I don't believe it!

> *(Then immediately controlling herself and forcing a laugh.)*

I mean, Ned was always so serious-minded it's hard to imagine him messed up in that sort of thing.

> *(Thinking in a queer state of jealous confusion.)*
> Hard to imagine! . . . my lover! . . . oh, pain again! . . . why? . . . I don't love him now . . . be careful! . . . Charlie's staring at me. . . .

MARSDEN

> *(Thinking – jealously.)*
> Then she did love him! . . . does she still? . . .
> *(Hopefully.)*

Or is it only pique? . . . no woman likes to lose a man even when she no longer loves him. . . .
>   (*With malicious insistence.*)

Why is that hard to imagine, Nina? Darrell never struck me as a Galahad. After all, why shouldn't he have a mistress?

>   (*Meaningly.*)

He has no tie over here to remain faithful to, has he?

NINA

>   (*Struggling with herself – thinking pitiably.*)
>   He's right . . . why shouldn't Ned? . . is that why he's never written? . . .
>   (*Airily.*)

I don't know what ties he has or hasn't got. It's nothing to me if he has fifty mistresses. I suppose he's no better than the rest of you.

EVANS

>   (*Looking over at her – tenderly reproachful.*)

That isn't fair, Nina.

>   (*Thinking-proudly.*)
>   I'm proud of that . . . never anyone before her . . .

NINA

>   (*Looking at him – with real gratitude.*)

I didn't mean you, dear.

>   (*Thinking – proudly.*)
>   Thank God for Sammy! . . . I know he's mine . . . no jealousy . . . no fear . . . no pain . . . I've found peace . . .
>   (*Then distractedly.*)

199

Oh, Ned, why haven't you written? . . . stop it! . . . what a fool I am! . . . Ned's dead for me! . . . oh, I hate Charlie! . . . why did he tell me? . . .

MARSDEN

(*Looking at Evans – contemptuously thinking.*)
What a poor simpleton Sam is! . . . boasting of his virtue! . . . as if women loved you for that! . . . they despise it! . . . I don't want Nina to think I've had no experiences with women. . . .
(*Mockingly.*)

So then it's Sam who is the Galahad, eh? Really, Nina, you should have him put in the Museum among the prehistoric mammals!

EVANS

(*Pleased – comes back teasingly.*)

Well, I never had your chances, Charlie! I couldn't run over to Europe and get away with murder the way you have!

MARSDEN

(*Foolishly pleased – admitting while denying.*)

Oh, I wasn't quite as bad as all that, Sam!

(*Scornfully ashamed of himself – thinking.*)
Poor sick ass that I am! . . . I want them to think I've been a Don Juan! . . . how pitiful and disgusting! . . . I wouldn't have a mistress if I could! . . . if I could? . . . of course I could! . . . I've simply never cared to degrade myself! . . .

NINA

(*Thinking – tormentedly.*)
The thought of that woman! . . . Ned forgetting our afternoons in nights with her! . . . stop these thoughts!

. . . I won't give in to them! . . . why did Charlie want to
hurt me? . . . is he jealous of Ned? . . . Charlie has always
loved me in some queer way of his own . . . how ridiculous!
. . . look at him! . . . he's so proud of being thought a Don
Juan! . . I'm sure he never even dared to kiss a woman
except his mother! . . .

> (*Mockingly.*)

Do tell us about all your various mistresses in foreign parts,
Charlie!

MARSDEN

> (*In confusion now.*)

I – I really don't remember, Nina!

NINA

Why, you're the most heartless person I've ever heard of,
Charlie! Not remember even one! And I suppose there are
little Marsdens – and you've forgotten all about them, too!

> (*She laughs maliciously – Evans laughs with her.*)

MARSDEN

> (*Still more confused – with a silly idiotic smirk.*)

I can't say about that, Nina. It's a wise father who knows
his own child, you know!

NINA

> (*Frightenedly – thinking.*)
> What does he mean? . . . does he suspect about the baby,
> too? . . . I must be terribly careful of Charlie! . . .

EVANS

> (*Looking up from his paper again.*)

Did Ned say anything about coming back?

NINA

(*Thinking – longingly.*)
Come back? . . . oh, Ned, how I wish! . . .

MARSDEN

(*Looking at her – meaningly.*)

No, he didn't say. I gathered he was staying over indefinitely.

EVANS

I'd sure like to see him again.

NINA

(*Thinking.*)
He has forgotten me . . . if he did come, he'd probably avoid me. . . .

MARSDEN

He spoke of you. He asked if I'd heard whether Nina had had her baby yet or not. I told him I hadn't.

EVANS

(*Heartily.*)

Too bad you didn't know. You could have told him what a world-beater we've got! Eh, Nina?

NINA

(*Mechanically.*)

Yes.

(*Joyfully – thinking.*)
Ned asked about my baby! . . . then he hadn't forgotten!
. . . if he came back he'd come to see his baby! . . .

STRANGE INTERLUDE

EVANS

(Solicitously.)

Isn't it time to nurse him again?

NINA

(Starts to her feet automatically.)

Yes, I'm going now.

(She glances at Marsden, thinking calculatingly.)
I must win Charlie over again . . . I don't feel safe . . .
*(She stops by his chair and takes his hand and looks
into his eyes gently and reproachfully.)*

MARSDEN

(Thinking shamefacedly.)
Why have I been trying to hurt her? . . . my Nina! . . .
I am nearer to her than anyone! . . . I'd give my life to
make her happy! . . .

NINA

(Triumphantly.)
How his hand trembles! . . . what a fool to be afraid of
Charlie! . . . I can always twist him round my finger! . . .
*(She runs her hand through his hair, and speaks as
though she were hiding a hurt reproach beneath
a joking tone.)*

I shouldn't like you any more, you know, after you've
practically admitted you've philandered all over Europe!
And I thought you were absolutely true to me, Charlie!

MARSDEN

(So pleased he can hardly believe his ears.)
Then she did believe me! . . . she's actually hurt! . . .
but I can't let her think . . .

(*With passionate earnestness, clasping her hand in both of his, looking into her eyes.*)

No, Nina! I swear to you!

NINA

(*Thinking – cruelly.*)

Pah! . . . how limp his hands are! . . . his eyes are so shrinking! . . . is it possible he loves me? . . . like that? . . . what a sickening idea! . . . it seems incestuous some-how! . . . no, it's too absurd! . . .

(*Smiling, gently releases her hand.*)

All right. I forgive you, Charlie.

(*Then matter-of-factly.*)

Excuse me, please, while I go up and feed my infant, or we're due to hear some lusty howling in a moment.

(*She turns away, then impulsively turns back and kisses Marsden with real affection.*)

You're an old dear, do you know it, Charlie? I don't know what I'd do without you!

(*Thinking.*)

It's true, too! . . . he's my only dependable friend . . . I must never lose him . . . never let him suspect about little Gordon . . .

(*She turns to go.*)

EVANS

(*Jumping up, throwing his paper aside.*)

Wait a second. I'll come with you. I want to say good night to him.

(*He comes, puts his arm about her waist, kisses her and they go out together.*)

MARSDEN

(*Thinking excitedly.*)

I almost confessed I loved her! . . . a queer expression came over her face . . . what was it? . . . was it satisfaction? . . . she didn't mind? . . . was it pleasure? . . . then I can hope? . . .

(*Then miserably.*)

Hope for what? . . . what do I want? . . . If Nina were free, what would I do? . . . would I do anything? . . . would I wish to? . . . what would I offer her? . . . money? . . . she could get that from others . . . myself? . . .

(*Bitterly.*)

What a prize! . . . my ugly body . . . there's nothing in me to attract her . . . my fame? . . . God, what a shoddy, pitiful! . . . but I might have done something big . . . I might still . . . if I had the courage to write the truth . . . but I was born afraid . . . afraid of myself . . . I've given my talent to making fools feel pleased with themselves in order that they'd feel pleased with me . . . and like me . . . I'm neither hated nor loved . . . I'm liked . . . women like me . . . Nina likes me! . . .

(*Resentfully.*)

She can't help letting the truth escape her! . . . "You're an old dear, do you know it, Charlie?" Oh, yes, I know it . . . too damned well! . . . dear old Charlie! . . .

(*In anguish.*)

Dear old Rover, nice old doggie, we've had him for years, he's so affectionate and faithful, but he's growing old, he's getting cross, we'll have to get rid of him soon! . . .

(*In a strange rage, threateningly.*)

But you won't get rid of me so easily, Nina! . . .

(*Then confusedly and shamefacedly.*)

Good God, what's the matter with me! . . . since Mother's death I've become a regular idiot! . . .

EVANS

(*Comes back from the right, a beaming look of proud parenthood on his face.*)

He was sleeping so soundly an earthquake wouldn't have made him peep!

(*He goes back to his chair – earnestly.*)

He sure is healthy and husky, Charlie. That tickles me more than anything else. I'm going to start in training him as soon as he's old enough – so he'll be a crack athlete when he goes to college – what I wanted to be and couldn't. I want him to justify the name of Gordon and be a bigger star than Gordon ever was, if that's possible.

MARSDEN

(*With a sort of pity – thinking.*)
His is an adolescent mind . . . he'll never grow up . . well, in this adolescent country, what greater blessing could he wish for? . . .
(*Forcing a smile.*)

How about training his mind?

EVANS

(*Confidently.*)

Oh, that'll take care of itself. Gordon was always near the top in his studies, wasn't he? And with Nina for a mother, his namesake ought to inherit a full set of brains.

MARSDEN

(*Amused.*)

You're the only genuinely modest person I know, Sam.

EVANS

(*Embarrassed.*)

Oh – me – I'm the boob of the family

(*Then hastily.*)

206

Except when it comes to business. I'll make the money.

(*Confidently.*)

And you can bet your sweet life I will make it!

MARSDEN

I'm quite sure of that.

EVANS

(*Very seriously – in a confidential tone.*)

I couldn't have said that two years ago – and believed it. I've changed a hell of a lot! Since the baby was born, I've felt as if I had a shot of dynamite in each arm. They can't pile on the work fast enough.

(*He grins – then seriously.*)

It was about time I got hold of myself. I wasn't much for Nina to feel proud about having around the house in those days. Now – well – at least I've improved. I'm not afraid of my own shadow any more.

MARSDEN

(*Thinking strangely.*)

Not to be afraid of one's shadow! . . . that must be the highest happiness of heaven! . . .

(*Flatteringly.*)

Yes, you've done wonders in the past year.

EVANS

Oh, I haven't even started yet. Wait till I get my chance!

(*Glances at Marsden sharply, makes up his mind and leans forward toward him confidentially.*)

And I see my real chance, Charlie – lying right ahead,

waiting for me to grab it – an agency that's been allowed to run down and go to seed. Within a year or so they'll be willing to sell out cheap. One of their people who's become a good pal of mine told me that in confidence, put it up to me. He'd take it on himself but he's sick of the game. But I'm not! I love it! It's great sport!

> (*Then putting the brake on this exuberance – matter-of-factly.*)

But I'll need a hundred thousand – and where will I get it?

> (*Looking at Marsden keenly, but putting on a joking tone.*)

Any suggestion you can make, Charlie, will be gratefully received.

MARSDEN

> (*Thinking suspiciously.*)
> Does he actually imagine I . . . ? and a hundred thousand, no less! . . . over one-fifth of my entire . . . by Jove, I'll have to throw cold water on that fancy! . . .
> (*Shortly.*)

No, Sam, I can't think of anyone. Sorry.

EVANS

> (*Without losing any confidence – with a grin.*)
> Check! . . . That's that! . . . Charlie's out . . . till the next time! . . . but I'll keep after him! . . .
> (*Contemplating himself with pride.*)
> Gee, I have changed all right! I can remember when a refusal like that would have ruined my confidence for six months!
> (*Heartily.*)

Nothing to be sorry about, old man. I only mentioned it on the off chance you might know of someone.

(*Trying a bold closing stroke – jokingly.*)

Why don't you be my partner, Charlie? Never mind the hundred thousand. We'll get that elsewhere. I'll bet you might have darn fine original ideas to contribute.

(*Thinking – satisfied.*)

There! . . . That'll keep my proposition pinned up in his mind! . . .

(*Then jumping to his feet – briskly.*)

What do you say to a little stroll down to the shore and back? Come on – do you good.

(*Taking his arm and hustling him genially toward the door.*)

What you need is exercise. You're soft as putty. Why don't you take up golf?

MARSDEN

(*With sudden resistance pulls away – determinedly.*)

No, I won't go, Sam. I want to think out a new plot.

EVANS

Oh, all right! If it's a case of work, go to it! See you later.

(*He goes out. A moment later the front door is heard closing.*)

MARSDEN

(*Looks after him with a mixture of annoyance and scornful amusement.*)

What a fount of meaningless energy he's tapped! . . .

always on the go . . . typical terrible child of the age . . .
universal slogan, keep moving . . . moving where? . . .
never mind that . . . don't think of ends . . . the means are
the end . . . keep moving! . . .

> (*He laughs scornfully and sits down in Evans' chair,
> picking up the paper and glancing at it sneer-
> ingly.*)

It's in every headline of this daily newer testament . . .
going . . . going . . . never mind the gone . . . we won't
live to see it . . . and we'll be so rich, we can buy off the
deluge, anyway! . . . even our new God has His price! . . .
must have! . . . aren't we made in His image? . . . or vice
versa? . .

> (*He laughs again, letting the paper drop disdainfully
> – then bitterly.*)

But why am I so superior? . . . where am I going? . . .
to the same nowhere! . . . worse! . . . I'm not even going!
. . I'm there! . . .

> (*He laughs with bitter self-pity – then begins to think
> with amused curiosity.*)

Become Sam's partner? . . . there's a grotesque notion!
. . . it might revive my sense of humour about myself, at
least . . . I'm the logical one to help him . . . I helped him
to Nina . . . logical partner . . . partner in Nina? . . .
what inane thoughts! . . .

> (*With a sigh.*)

No use trying to think out that plot to-night . . . I'll try
to read. . . .

> (*He sees the book he has been reading on the couch and
> gets up to get it. There is a ring from the front
> door. Marsden turns toward it uncertainly. A
> pause. Then Nina's voice calls down the stairs.*)

NINA

The maid's out. Will you go to the door, Charlie?

STRANGE INTERLUDE

MARSDEN

Surely.

> (*He goes out and opens the front door. A pause.
> Then he can be heard saying resentfully:*)

Hallo, Darrell.

> (*And some one answering "Hallo, Marsden." and
> coming in and the door closing.*)

NINA

> (*From upstairs, her voice strange and excited.*)

Who is it, Charlie?

DARRELL

> (*Comes into view in the hall, opposite the doorway, at
> the foot of the stairs – his voice trembling a little
> with suppressed emotion.*)

It's I, Nina – Ned Darrell.

NINA

> (*With a glad cry.*)

Ned!

> (*Then in a voice which shows she is trying to control
> herself, and is frightened now.*)

I – make yourself at home. I'll be down – in a minute or
two.

> (*Darrell remains standing looking up the stairs in a
> sort of joyous stupor. Marsden stares at him.*)

MARSDEN

> (*Sharply.*)

Come on in and sit down.

(Darrell starts, comes into the room, plainly getting a grip on himself. Marsden follows him, glaring at his back with enmity and suspicion. Darrell moves as far away from him as possible, sitting down on the sofa at right. Marsden takes Evans' chair by the table. Darrell is pale, thin, nervous, unhealthy looking. There are lines of desperation in his face, puffy shadows of dissipation and sleeplessness under his restless, harried eyes. He is dressed carelessly, almost shabbily. His eyes wander about the room, greedily taking it in.)

DARRELL

(Thinking disjointedly.)

Here again! . . . dreamed of this house . . . from here, ran away . . . I've come back . . . my turn to be happy! . . .

MARSDEN

(Watching him – savagely.)

Now I know! . . . absolutely! . . . his face! . . . her voice! . . . they did love each other! . . . they do now! . . .
(Sharply.)

When did you get back from Europe?

DARRELL

(Curtly.)

This morning on the "Olympic."

(Thinking – cautiously.)

Look out for this fellow . . . always had it in for me . . . like a woman . . . smells out love . . . he suspected before . . .

(Then boldly.)

Well, who gives a damn now? . . . all got to come out!
. . . Nina wanted to tell Sam . . . now I'll tell him myself! . . .

MARSDEN

(*Righteously indignant.*)

What has brought him back? . . . what a devilish, cowardly trick to play on poor unsuspecting Sam! . . .

(*Revengefully.*)

But I'm not unsuspecting! . . . I'm not their fool! . . .

(*Coldly.*)

What brought you back so soon? When I saw you in
Munich you weren't intending –

DARRELL

(*Shortly.*)

My father died three weeks ago. I've had to come back
about his estate.

(*Thinking.*)

Lie . . . Father's death just gave me an excuse to myself
. . . wouldn't have come back for that . . . came back
because I love her! . . . damn his questions! . . . I want to
think . . . before I see her . . . sound of her voice . . .
seemed to burn inside my head . . . God, I'm licked! . . .
no use fighting it . . . I've done my damnedest . . . work
. . . booze . . . other women . . . no use . . . I love her!
. . . always! . . . to hell with pride! . . .

MARSDEN

(*Thinking.*)

He has two brothers . . . they'll probably all share
equally . . . his father noted Philadelphia surgeon . . . rich,
I've heard . . .

(*With a bitter grin.*)

Wait till Sam hears that! . . . he'll ask Darrell to back him . . . and Darrell will jump at it . . . chance to avert suspicion . . . conscience money, too! . . . it's my duty to protect Sam . . .

> (*As he hears Nina coming down the stairs.*)

I must watch them . . . it's my duty to protect Nina from herself . . . Sam is a simpleton . . . I'm all she has . . .

DARRELL

> (*Hearing her coming – in a panic – thinking.*)

Coming! . . . in a second I'll see her! . . .

> (*Terrified.*)

Does she still love me? . . . she may have forgotten . . . no, it's my child . . . she can never forget that! . . .

> (*Nina comes in from the rear. She has put on a fresh dress, her hair is arranged, her face newly rouged and powdered, she looks extremely pretty and this is heightened by the feverish state of mind she is in – a mixture of love, of triumphant egotism in knowing her lover has come back to her, and of fear and uncertainty in feeling her new peace, her certainties, her contented absorption in her child failing her. She hesitates just inside the door, staring into Darrell's eyes, thinking a fierce question.*)

NINA

Does he still love me? . . .

> (*Then triumphantly as she reads him.*)

Yes! . . . he does! . . . he does! . . .

DARRELL

> (*Who has jumped to his feet – with a cry of longing.*)

Nina!

> (*Thinking with alarm now.*)

214

She's changed! . . . changed! . . . can't tell if she loves! . . .

>   (*He has started to go to her. Now he hesitates.*)
>   (*His voice taking on a pleading uncertain quality.*)

Nina!

NINA

>   (*Thinking triumphantly – with a certain cruelty.*)
>   He loves me! . . . he's mine . . . now more than ever!
>   . . . he'll never dare leave me again! . . .
>   (*Certain of herself now, she comes to him and speaks
>   with confident pleasure.*)

Hallo, Ned! This is a wonderful surprise! How are you?

>   (*She takes his hand.*)

DARRELL

>   (*Taken aback – confusedly.*)

Oh – all right, Nina.

>   (*Thinking in a panic.*)
>   That tone! . . . as if she didn't care! . . . can't believe
>   that! . . she's playing a game to fool Marsden! . . .

MARSDEN

>   (*Who is watching them keenly – thinking.*)
>   She loves his love for her . . . she's cruelly confident . . .
>   much as I hate this man I can't help feeling sorry . . . I
>   know her cruelty . . . it's time I took a hand in this . . .
>   what a plot for a novel! . . .
>   (*Almost mockingly.*)

Darrell's father died, Nina. He had to come home to see about the estate.

DARRELL

(*With a glare at Marsden – protestingly.*)

I was coming home anyway. I only intended to stay a year, and it's over that since –

(*Intensely.*)

I was coming back anyway, Nina!

NINA

(*Thinking with triumphant happiness.*)
You dear, you! . . . as if I didn't know that! . . oh, how I'd love to take you in my arms! . . .
(*Happily.*)

I'm awfully glad you've come, Ned. We've missed you terribly.

DARRELL

(*Thinking – more and more at sea.*)
She looks glad . . . but she's changed . . . I don't understand her . . . "we've missed" . . . that means Sam . . what does that mean? . . .
(*Intensely, pressing her hand.*)

And I've missed you – terribly!

MARSDEN

(*Sardonically.*)

Yes, indeed, Darrell, I can vouch for their missing you – Sam in particular. He was asking about you only a short while ago – how things were going with you when I saw you in Munich.

(*Maliciously.*)

By the way, who was the lady you were with that day? She was certainly startling-looking.

NINA

(*Thinking – triumphantly mocking.*)
A miss, Charlie! . . . he loves me! . . . what do I care
about that woman? . . .
(*Gaily.*)

Yes, who was the mysterious beauty, Ned? Do tell us!

(*She moves away from him and sits down at centre.
Darrell remains standing.*)

DARRELL

(*Glaring at Marsden, sullenly.*)

Oh, I don't remember –

(*Thinking apprehensively with a bitter resentment.*)
She doesn't give a damn! . . . if she loved me she'd be
jealous! . . . but she doesn't give a damn! . . .
(*He blurts out resentfully at Nina.*)

Well, she was my mistress – for a time – I was lonely.

(*Then with sudden anger, turning on Marsden.*)

But what's all this to you, Marsden?

MARSDEN

(*Coolly.*)

Absolutely nothing. Pardon me. It was a tactless question.

(*Then with continued open malice.*)

But I was starting to say how Sam had missed you, Darrell.
It's really remarkable. One doesn't encounter such friendship often in these slack days. Why, he'd trust you with
anything!

NINA

(*Wincing – thinking.*)
That hurts . . . hurts Ned . . . Charlie is being cruel! . . .

DARRELL

(*Wincing – in a forced tone.*)
And I'd trust Sam with anything.

MARSDEN

Of course. He is a person one can trust. They are rare. You're going to be amazed at the change in Sam, Darrell. Isn't he, Nina? He's a new man. I never saw such energy. If ever a man was bound for success Sam is. In fact, I'm so confident he is that as soon as he thinks the time is ripe to start his own firm I'm going to furnish the capital and become his silent partner.

DARRELL

(*Puzzled and irritated – thinking confusedly.*)
What's he driving at? . . . why the hell doesn't he get out and leave us alone? . . . but I'm glad Sam is on his feet . . . makes it easier to tell him the truth. . . .

NINA

(*Thinking – worriedly.*)
What's Charlie talking about? . . . it's time I talked to Ned . . . Oh, Ned, I do love you! . . . you can be my lover! . . . we won't hurt Sam! . . . he'll never know! . . .

MARSDEN

Yes, ever since the baby was born Sam's been another man – in fact, ever since he knew there was going to be a baby, isn't it, Nina?

NINA

(Agreeing as if she had only half heard him.)

Yes.

(Thinking.)
Ned's baby! . . . I must talk to him about our baby. . . .

MARSDEN

Sam is the proudest parent I've ever seen!

NINA

(As before.)

Yes, Sam makes a wonderful father, Ned.

(Thinking.)
Ned doesn't care for children . . . I know what you're hoping, Ned . . . but if you think I'm going to take Sam's baby from him, you're mistaken! . . . or if you think I'll run away with you and leave my baby . . .

MARSDEN

(With the same strange driving insistence.)

If anything happened to that child I actually believe Sam would lose his reason! Don't you think so, Nina?

NINA

(With emphasis.)

I know I'd lose mine! Little Gordon has become my whole life.

DARRELL

(Thinking – with a sad bitter irony.)
Sam . . . wonderful father . . . lose his reason . . . little Gordon! . . . Nina called my son after Gordon! . . roman-

tic imagination! . . . Gordon is still her lover! . . Gordon, Sam and Nina! . . . and my son! . . . closed corporation! . . . I'm forced out! . . .

(*Then rebelling furiously.*)

No! . . . not yet, by God! . . . I'll smash it up! . . . I'll tell Sam the truth no matter what! . . .

NINA

(*Thinking with a strange calculation.*)

I couldn't find a better husband than Sam . . . and I couldn't find a better lover than Ned . . . I need them both to be happy . . .

MARSDEN

(*With sudden despairing suspicion.*)

Good God . . after all, is it Sam's child? . . . mightn't it be Darrell's! . . . why have I never thought of that? . . No! . . . Nina couldn't be so vile! . . . to go on living with Sam, pretending . . . and, after all, why should she, you fool? . . . there's no sense! . . . she could have gone off with Darrell, couldn't she? . . . Sam would have given her a divorce . . . there was no possible reason for her staying with Sam, when she loved Darrell, unless exactly because this was Sam's baby . . . for its sake . . .

(*Hectically relieved.*)

Of course! . . . of course! . . . that's all right! . . . I love that poor baby now! . . . I'll fight for its sake against these two! . . .

(*Smilingly gets to his feet – thinking.*)

I can leave them alone now . . . for they won't be alone, thanks to me! . . . I leave Sam and his baby in this room with them . . . and their honour . . .

(*Suddenly raging.*)

Their honour! . . . what an obscene joke! . . . the honour of a harlot and a pimp! . . . I hate them! . . . if only God would strike them dead! . . . now! . . . and I could see them die! . . . I would praise His justice! . . . His kindness and mercy to me! . . .

STRANGE INTERLUDE

NINA

(*Thinking – with horrified confusion.*)
Why doesn't Charlie go? . . . What is he thinking? . . .
I suddenly feel afraid of him! . . .
(*She gets to her feet with a confused pleading cry.*)

Charlie!

MARSDEN

(*Immediately urbane and smiling.*)

It's all right. I'm going out to find Sam. When he knows
you're here he'll come on the run, Darrell.

(*He goes to the door. They watch him suspiciously.*)

And you two probably have a lot to talk over.

(*He chuckles pleasantly and goes into the hall –
mockingly warning.*)

We'll be back before long.

(*The front door is heard slamming. Nina and Darrell
turn and look at each other guiltily and frightenedly. Then he comes to her and takes both of
her hands uncertainly.*)

DARRELL

(*Stammeringly.*)

Nina – I – I've come back to you – do you – do you still
care – Nina?

NINA

(*Giving way to his love passionately, as if to drown
her fears.*)

I love you, Ned!

DARRELL

(Kisses her awkwardly – stammering.)

I – I didn't know – you seemed so cold – damn Marsden! – he suspects, doesn't he? – but it makes no difference now, does it?

(Then in a flood of words.)

Oh, it's been hell, Nina! I couldn't forget you! Other women – they only made me love you more! I hated them and loved you even at the moment when – that's honest! It was always you in my arms – as you used to be – those afternoons – God, how I've thought of them – lying awake – recalling every word you said, each movement, each expression on your face, smelling your hair, feeling your soft body –

(Suddenly taking her in his arms and kissing her again and again – passionately.)

Nina! I love you so!

NINA

And I've longed for you so much! Do you think I've forgotten those afternoons?

(Then in anguish.)

Oh, Ned, why did you run away? I can never forgive that! I can never trust you again!

DARRELL

(Violently.)

I was a fool! I thought of Sam! And that wasn't all! Oh, I wasn't all noble, I'll confess! I thought of myself and my career! Damn my career! A lot of good that did it! I didn't study! I didn't live! I longed for you – and suffered! I paid in full, believe me, Nina! But I know better now! I've come back. The time for lying is past! You've got to come away with me!

(*He kisses her.*)

NINA

(*Letting herself go, kissing him passionately.*)

Yes! My lover!

(*Then suddenly resisting and pushing him away.*)

No! You're forgetting Sam – and Sam's baby!

DARRELL

(*Staring at her wildly.*)

Sam's baby? Are you joking? Ours, you mean! We'll take him with us, of course!

NINA

(*Sadly.*)

And Sam?

DARRELL

Damn Sam! He's got to give you a divorce! Let him be generous for a change!

NINA

(*Sadly but determinedly.*)

He would be. You must be just to Sam. He'd give his life for my happiness. And this would mean his life. Could we be happy then? You know we couldn't! And I've changed, Ned. You've got to realize that. I'm not your old mad

223

Nina. I still love you. I shall always love you. But now I love my baby, too. His happiness comes first with me!

DARRELL

But – he's mine, too!

NINA

No! You gave him to Sam to save Sam!

DARRELL

To hell with Sam! It was to make you happy!

NINA

So I could make Sam happy! That was in it, too! I was sincere in that, Ned! If I hadn't been, I could never have gone to you that first day – or if I had, I'd never have forgiven myself. But as it is I don't feel guilty or wicked. I have made Sam happy! and I'm proud! I love Sam's happiness! I love the devoted husband and father in him! And I feel it's his baby – that we've made it his baby!

DARRELL

(*Distractedly.*)

Nina! For God's sake! You haven't come to love Sam, have you! Then – I'll go – I'll go away again – I'll never come back – I tried not to this time – but I had to, Nina!

NINA

(*Taking him in her arms – with sudden alarm.*)

No, don't go away, Ned – ever again. I don't love Sam! I love you!

DARRELL

(*Miserably.*)

But I don't understand! Sam gets everything – and I have nothing!

NINA

You have my love!

(*With a strange, self-assured smile at him.*)

It seems to me you're complaining unreasonably!

DARRELL

You mean – I can be – your lover again?

NINA

(*Simply, even matter-of-factly.*)

Isn't that the nearest we can come to making everyone happy? That's all that counts.

DARRELL

(*With a harsh laugh.*)

And is that what you call playing fair to Sam?

NINA

(*Simply.*)

Sam will never know. The happiness I have given him has made him too sure of himself ever to suspect me now. And as long as we can love each other without danger to him, I feel he owes that to us for all we've done for him.

(*With finality.*)

That's the only possible solution, Ned, for all our sakes, now you've come back to me.

DARRELL

(*Repulsed.*)

Nina! How can you be so inhuman and calculating!

NINA

(*Stung – mockingly.*)

It was you who taught me the scientific approach, Doctor!

DARRELL

(*Shrinking back from her – threateningly.*)

Then I'll leave again! I'll go back to Europe! I won't endure –!

(*Then in a queer, futile rage.*)

You think I'll stay – to be your lover – watching Sam with my wife and my child – you think that's what I came back to you for? You can go to hell, Nina!

NINA

(*Calmly – sure of him.*)

But what else can I do, Ned?

(*Then warningly.*)

I hear them coming, dear. It's Sam, you know.

DARRELL

(*In a frenzy.*)

What else can you do? Liar! But I can do something else!

226

I can smash your calculating game for you! I can tell Sam —
and I will — right now — by God, I will!

NINA

(*Quietly.*)

No. You won't, Ned. You can't do that to Sam.

DARRELL

(*Savagely.*)

Like hell I can't!

(*The front door is opened. Evans' voice is immediately heard, even before he bounds into the room.
He rushes up to Ned hilariously, shakes his hand
and pounds his back, oblivious of Darrell's wild
expression.*)

EVANS

You old son of a gun! Why didn't you let a guy know you
were coming? We'd have met you at the dock, and brought
the baby. Let me have a look at you! You look thinner.
We'll fatten you up, won't we, Nina? Let us do the prescribing this time! Why didn't you let us know where you were,
you old bum? We wanted to write you about the baby. And
I wanted to boast about how I was getting on! You're the
only person in the world — except Nina and Charlie — I would
boast about that to.

NINA

(*Affectionately.*)

Mercy, Sam, give Ned a chance to get a word in!

(*Looking at Ned pityingly but challengingly.*)

He wants to tell you something, Sam.

STRANGE INTERLUDE

DARRELL

(Crushed – stammers.)

No – I mean, yes – I want to tell you how damn glad I
am . . .

> *(He turns away, his face is screwed up in his effort to
> hold back his tears.)*
> *(Thinking miserably.)*
> I can't tell him! . . . God damn him, I can't! . . .

NINA

> *(With a strange triumphant calm.)*
> There! . . . that's settled for all time! . . . poor Ned!
> . . . how crushed he looks! . . . I mustn't let Sam look at
> him! . . .
> *(She steps between them protectingly.)*

Where's Charlie, Sam?

MARSDEN

> *(Appearing from the hall.)*

Here, Nina. Always here!

> *(He comes to her, smiling with assurance.)*

NINA

> *(Suddenly with a strange unnatural elation – looking
> from one to the other with triumphant posses-
> sion.)*

Yes, you're here, Charlie – always! And you, Sam – and
Ned!

> *(With a strange gaiety.)*

228

Sit down, all of you! Make yourselves at home! You are my three men! This is your home with me!

(*Then in a strange half-whisper.*)

Ssshh! I thought I heard the baby. You must all sit down and be very quiet. You must not wake our baby.

> (*Mechanically the three sit down, careful to make no noise — Evans in his old place by the table, Marsden at centre, Darrell on the sofa at right. They sit staring before them in silence. Nina remains standing, dominating them, a little behind and to the left of Marsden.*)

DARRELL

(*Thinking abjectly.*)

I couldn't! . . . there are things one may not do and live with oneself afterwards . . . there are things one may not say . . . memory is too full of echoes! . . . there are secrets one must not reveal . . . memory is lined with mirrors! . . . he was too happy! . . . to kill happiness is a worse murder than taking life! . . . I gave him that happiness! . . . Sam deserves my happiness! . . . God bless you, Sam! . . .

(*Then in a strange objective tone — thinking.*)

My experiment with the guinea-pigs has been a success . . . the ailing ones, Sam, and the female, Nina, have been restored to health and normal function . . . only the other male, Ned, seems to have suffered deterioration. . . .

(*Then bitterly humble.*)

Nothing left but to accept her terms . . . I love her . . . I can help to make her happy . . . half a loaf is better . . . to a starving man. . . .

(*Glancing over at Evans — bitterly gloating.*)

And your child is mine! . . . your wife is mine! . . . your happiness is mine! . . . may you enjoy my happiness, her husband! . . .

EVANS

(Looking at Darrell affectionately.)

Sure good to see Ned again . . . a real friend if there ever
was one . . . looks blue about something . . . oh, that's
right, Charlie said his old man had kicked in . . . his old
man was rich . . . that's an idea . . . I'll bet he'd put up
that capital . . .

(Then ashamed of himself.)

Aw hell, what's the matter with me? . . . he's no sooner
here than I start . . . he's done enough . . . forget it! . . .
now, anyway . . . he looks pretty dissipated . . . too many
women . . . ought to get married and settle down . . . tell
him that if I didn't think he'd laugh at me giving him advice
. . . but he'll soon realize I'm not the old Sam he knew . . .
I suppose Nina's been boasting about that already . . . she's
proud . . . she's helped me . . . she's a wonderful wife and
mother . . .

(Looking up at her – solicitously.)

She acted a bit nervous just now . . . queer . . . like she
used to . . . haven't noticed her that way for a long time . . .
suppose it's the excitement of Ned turning up . . . mustn't
let her get over-excited . . . bad for the baby's milk. . . .

MARSDEN

*(Glancing furtively over his shoulder at Nina –
broodingly thinking.)*

She's the old queer Nina now . . . the Nina I could never
fathom . . . her three men! . . . and we are! . . . I? . . .
yes, more deeply than either of the others since I serve for
nothing . . . a queer kind of love, maybe . . . I am not
ordinary! . . . our child . . . what could she mean by that?
. . . child of us three? . . . on the surface, that's insane . . .
but I felt when she said it there was something in it . . . she
has strange devious intuitions that tap the hidden currents
of life . . . dark intermingling currents that become the one
stream of desire . . . I feel, with regard to Nina, my life

queerly identified with Sam's and Darrell's . . . her child is the child of our three loves for her . . . I would like to believe that . . . I would like to be her husband in a sense . . . and the father of a child, after my fashion . . . I could forgive her everything . . . permit everything . . .

(*Determinedly.*)

And I do forgive! . . . and I will not meddle hereafter more than is necessary to guard her happiness, and Sam's and our baby's . . . as for Darrell, I am no longer jealous of him . . . she is only using his love for her own happiness . . . he can never take her away from me! . . .

NINA

(*More and more strangely triumphant.*)

My three men! . . . I feel their desires converge in me! . . . to form one complete beautiful male desire which I absorb . . . and am whole . . . they dissolve in me, their life is my life . . . I am pregnant with the three! . . . husband! . . . lover! . . . father! . . . and the fourth man! . . . little man! . . . little Gordon! . . . he is mine, too! . . . that makes it perfect! . . .

(*With an extravagant suppressed exultance.*)

Why, I should be the proudest woman on earth! . . . I should be the happiest woman in the world! . . .

(*Then suppressing an outbreak of hysterical triumphant laughter only by a tremendous effort.*)

Ha-ha . . . only I better knock wood . . .

(*She raps with both knuckles in a fierce tattoo on the table.*)

before God the Father hears my happiness! . . .

EVANS

(*As the three turn to her – anxiously.*)

Nina? What's the matter?

NINA

(*Controlling herself with a great effort comes to him – forcing a smile – puts her arms around him affectionately.*)

Nothing, dear. Nerves, that's all. I'm over-tired, I guess.

EVANS

(*Bullying her – with loving authority.*)

Then you go right to bed, young lady! We'll excuse you.

NINA

(*Quietly and calmly now.*)

All right, dear. I guess I do need to rest.

(*She kisses him as she might kiss a big brother she loved – affectionately.*)

Good night, you bossy old thing, you!

EVANS

(*With deep tenderness.*)

Good night, darling.

NINA

(*She goes and kisses Charlie dutifully on the cheek as she might her father – affectionately.*)

Good night, Charlie.

MARSDEN

(*With a touch of her father's manner.*)

That's a good girl! Good night, dear.

NINA

(She goes and kisses Darrell lovingly on the lips as she would kiss her lover.)

Good night, Ned.

DARRELL

(Looks at her with grateful humility.)

Thank you. Good night.

(She turns and walks quietly out of the room. The eyes of the three men follow her.)

(Curtain.)

ACT SEVEN

SCENE: *Nearly eleven years later. The sitting-room of the Evans' apartment on Park Avenue, New York City – a room that is a tribute to Nina's good taste. It is a large, sunny room, the furniture expensive but extremely simple. The arrangement of the furniture shown is as in previous scenes except there are more pieces. Two chairs are by the table at left. There is a smaller table at centre, and a chaise longue. A large, magnificently comfortable sofa is at right.*

It is about one in the afternoon of a day in early fall. Nina and Darrell and their son, Gordon, are in the room. Nina is reclining on the chaise longue watching Gordon who is sitting on the floor near her, turning over the pages of a book. Darrell is sitting by the table at left, watching Nina.

Nina is thirty-five, in the full bloom of her womanhood. She is slimmer than in the previous scene. Her skin still retains a trace of summer tan and she appears in the pink of physical condition. But as in the first act of the play, there is beneath this a sense of great mental strain. One notices the many lines in her face at second glance. Her eyes are tragically sad in repose and her expression is set and mask-like.

Gordon is eleven – a fine boy with, even at this age, the figure of an athlete. He looks older than he is. There is a grave expression on his face. His eyes are full of a quick-tempered sensitiveness. He does not noticeably resemble his mother. He looks nothing at all like his father. He seems to have sprung from a line distinct from any of the people we have seen.

Darrell has aged greatly. His hair is streaked with grey.

234

He has grown stout. His face is a bit jowly and puffy under the eyes. The features have become blurred. He has the look of a man with no definite aim or ambition to which he can relate his living. His eyes are embittered and they hide his inner self-resentment behind a pose of cynical indifference.

GORDON

(Thinking – resentfully.)

I wish Darrell'd get out of here! . . . why couldn't Mother let me run my own birthday? . . . I'd never had him here, you bet! . . . what's he always hanging 'round for? . . . why don't he go off on one of his old trips again? . . . last time he was gone more'n a year . . . I was hoping he'd died! . . . what makes Mother like him so much? . . . she makes me sick! . . . I'd think she'd get sick of the old fool and tell him to get out and never come back! . . . I'd kick him out if I was big enough! . . . it's good for him he didn't bring me any birthday present or I'd smash it first chance I got! . . .

NINA

(Watching him – brooding with loving tenderness - sadly.)

No longer my baby . . . my little man . . . eleven . . . I can't believe it . . . I'm thirty-five . . . five years more . . . at forty a woman has finished living . . . life passes by her . . . she rots away in peace! . . .

(Intensely.)

I want to rot away in peace! . . . I'm sick of the fight for happiness! . . .

(Smiling with a wry amusement at herself.)

What ungrateful thoughts on my son's birthday! . . . my love for him has been happiness . . . how handsome he is! . . . not at all like Ned . . . when I was carrying him I was fighting to forget Ned . . . hoping he might be like Gordon

. . . and he is . . . poor Ned, I've made him suffer a great
deal . . . !

(*She looks over at Darrell – self-mockingly.*)

My lover! . . . so very rarely now, those interludes of
passion . . . what has bound us together all these years?
. . . love? . . . if he could only have been contented with
what I was able to give him! . . . but he has always wanted
more . . . yet never had the courage to insist on all or
nothing . . . proud without being proud enough! . . . he
has shared me for his comfort's sake with a little gratitude
and a big bitterness . . . and sharing me has corrupted
him! . . .

(*Then bitterly.*)

No, I can't blame myself! . . . no woman can make a
man happy who has no purpose in life! . . . why did he give
up his career? . . . because I had made him weak? . . .

(*With resentful scorn.*)

No, it was I who shamed him into taking up biology and
starting the station at Antigua . . . if I hadn't he'd simply
have hung around me year after year, doing nothing . . .

(*Irritatedly.*)

Why does he stay so long? . . . over six months . . . I
can't stand having him around me that long any more! . . .
why doesn't he go back to the West Indies? . . . I always
get a terrible feeling after he's been back a while that he's
waiting for Sam to die! . . . or go insane! . . .

DARRELL

(*Thinking – with an apathetic bitterness.*)

What is she thinking? . . . we sit together in silence,
thinking . . . thoughts that never know the other's thoughts
. . . our love has become the intimate thinking together of
thoughts that are strangers . . . our love! . . . well, whatever it is that has bound us together, it's strong! . . . I've
broken with her, run away, tried to forget her . . . running
away to come back each time more abject! . . . or, if she saw
there was some chance I might break loose, she'd find some
way to call me back . . . and I'd forget my longing for

freedom, I'd come wagging my tail . . . no, guinea-pigs have no tails . . . I hope my experiment has proved something! . . . Sam . . . happy and wealthy . . . and healthy! . . . I used to hope he'd break down . . . I'd watch him and read symptoms of insanity into every move he made . . . despicable? . . . certainly, but love makes one either noble or despicable! . . . he only grew healthier . . . now I've given up watching him . . . almost entirely . . . now I watch him grow fat and I laugh! . . . the huge joke has dawned on me! . . . Sam is the only normal one! . . . we lunatics! . . . Nina and I! . . . have made a sane life for him out of our madness! . . .

(*Watching Nina – sadly.*)

Always thinking of her son . . . well, I gave him to her . . . Gordon . . . I hate that name . . . why do I continue hanging around here? . . . each time after a few months my love changes to bitterness . . . I blame Nina for the mess I've made of life . . .

NINA

(*Suddenly turning on him.*)

When are you going back to the West Indies, Ned?

DARRELL

(*Determinedly.*)

Soon!

GORDON

(*Stops playing to listen – thinking.*)
Gosh, I'm glad! . . . How soon, I wonder? . . .

NINA

(*With a trace of a sneer.*)

I don't see how you can afford to leave your work for such long periods. Don't you grow rusty?

DARRELL

(*Looking at her meaningly.*)

My life work is to rust – nicely and unobtrusively!

(*He smiles mockingly.*)

NINA

(*Sadly – thinking.*)

To rot away in peace . . . that's all he wants now, too!
. . . and this is what love has done to us! . . .

DARRELL

(*Bitterly.*)

My work was finished twelve years ago. As I believe you
know, I ended it with an experiment which resulted so suc-
cessfully that any further meddling with human lives would
have been superfluous!

NINA

(*Pityingly.*)

Ned!

DARRELL

(*Indifferent and cynical.*)

But you meant my present dabbling about. You know
better than to call that work. It's merely my hobby. Our
backing Sam has made Marsden and me so wealthy that we're
forced to take up hobbies. Marsden goes in for his old one of
dashing off genteel novels, while I play at biology. Sam
argued that golf would be healthier and less nonsensical for
me, but you insisted on biology. And give it its due, it has
kept me out in the open air and been conducive to travelling
and broadening my mind!

(*Then forcing a smile.*)

But I'm exaggerating. I really am interested, or I'd never keep financing the Station. And when I'm down there I do work hard, helping Preston. He's doing remarkable work already, and he's still in his twenties. He'll be a big man —

(*His bitterness cropping up again.*)

at least if he takes my advice and never carries his experiments as far as human lives!

NINA

(*In a low voice.*)

How can you be so bitter, Ned — on Gordon's birthday?

DARRELL

(*Thinking cynically.*)

She expects me to love the child she deliberately took from me and gave to another man! . . . no, thank you, Nina! . . . I've been hurt enough! . . . I'll not leave myself open there! . . . .

(*Regarding his son bitterly.*)

Every day he gets more like Sam, doesn't he?

GORDON

(*Thinking.*)

He's talking about me . . . he better look out! . . .

NINA

(*Resentfully.*)

I don't think Gordon resembles Sam at all. He reminds me a great deal of his namesake.

239

DARRELL

(*Touched on a sore spot – with a nasty laugh – cuttingly.*)

Gordon Shaw? Not the slightest bit in the world! And you ought to thank God he doesn't! It's the last thing I'd wish for a boy of mine – to be like that rah-rah hero!

GORDON

(*Thinking contemptuously.*)
Boy of his! . . . He hasn't got a boy! . . .

NINA

(*Amused and pleased by his jealousy.*)
Poor Ned! . . . isn't he silly? . . . at his age, after all we've been through, to feel jealous still . . .

DARRELL

I'd much rather have him

(*Pointing to Gordon.*)

grow up to be an exact duplicate of the esteemed Samuel!

GORDON

(*Thinking resentfully.*)
He's always making fun of my father! . . he better look out! . . .

DARRELL

(*More and more mockingly.*)

And what could be fairer? The good Samuel is an A 1 success. He has a charming wife and a darling boy, and a

Park Avenue apartment and a membership in an expensive golf club. And, above all, he rests so complacently on the proud assurance that he is self-made!

NINA

(*Sharply.*)

Ned! You ought to be ashamed! You know how grateful Sam has always been to you!

DARRELL

(*Bitingly.*)

Would he be grateful if he knew how much I'd really done for him?

NINA

(*Sternly.*)

Ned!

GORDON

(*Suddenly jumps up and confronts Darrell, his fists clenched, trembling with rage, stammers.*)

You – shut up – making fun of my father!

NINA

(*In dismay.*)

Gordon!

DARRELL

(*Mockingly.*)

My dear boy, I wouldn't make fun of your father for the world!

241

GORDON

(*Baffledly – his lips trembling.*)

You – you did, too!

(*Then intensely.*)

I hate you!

NINA

(*Shocked and indignant.*)

Gordon! How dare you talk like that to your Uncle Ned!

GORDON

(*Rebelliously.*)

He's not my uncle! He's not my anything!

NINA

Not another word or you'll be punished, whether it's your birthday or not! If you can't behave better than that, I'll have to 'phone to all your friends they mustn't come here this afternoon, that you've been so bad you can't have a party!

(*Thinking remorsefully.*)

Is this my fault? . . . I've done my best to get him to love Ned! . . . but it only makes him worse! . . . it makes him turn against me! . . . turn from me to Sam! . . .

GORDON

(*Sullenly.*)

I don't care! I'll tell Dad!

242

NINA

(Peremptorily.)

Leave the room! And don't come near me again, do you hear, until you've apologized to Uncle Ned!

(Thinking angrily.)
Dad! . . . It's always Dad with him now! . . .

DARRELL

(Boredly.)

Oh, never mind, Nina!

GORDON

(Going out – mutters.)

I won't 'pologize – never!

(Thinking vindictively.)
I hate her too when she sides with him! . . . I don't care if she is my mother! . . . she has no right! . . .
(He goes out, rear.)

DARRELL

(Irritably.)

What if he does hate me? I don't blame him! He suspects what I know – that I've acted like a coward and a weakling toward him! I should have claimed him no matter what happened to other people! Whose fault is it if he hates me, and I dislike him because he loves another father? Ours! You gave him to Sam and I consented! All right! Then don't blame him for acting like Sam's son!

243

NINA

But he shouldn't say he hates you.

(*Thinking bitterly*.)

Sam's! . . . he's becoming all Sam's! . . . I'm getting to mean nothing! . . .

DARRELL

(*Sardonically*.)

Perhaps he realizes subconsciously that I am his father, his rival in your love; but I'm not his father ostensibly, there are no taboos, so he can come right out and hate me to his heart's content!

(*Bitterly*.)

If he realized how little you love me any more, he wouldn't bother!

NINA

(*Exasperatedly*.)

Oh, Ned, do shut up! I can't stand hearing those same old reproaches I've heard a thousand times before! I can't bear to hear myself making the same old bitter counter-accusations. And then there'll be the same old terrible scene of hate and you'll run away – it used to be to drink and women, now it's to the Station. Or I'll send you away, and then after a time I'll call you back, because I'll have got so lonely again living this lonely lie of my life, with no one to speak to except Sam's business friends and their deadly wives.

(*She laughs helplessly*.)

Or else you'll get lonely in your lie a little before I do and come back again of your own desire! And then we'll kiss and cry and love each other again!

DARRELL

(*With an ironical grimace.*)

Or I might cheat myself into believing I'd fallen in love with some nice girl and get myself engaged to be married again as I did once before! And then you'd be jealous again and have to find some way of getting me to break it off!

NINA

(*Forlornly amused.*)

Yes – I suppose the thought of a wife taking you away from me would be too much – again!

(*Then helplessly.*)

Oh, Ned, when are we ever going to learn something about each other? We act like such brainless fools – with our love. It's always so wonderful when you first come back, but you always stay too long – or I always keep you too long! You never leave before we've come to the ugly bitter stage when we blame each other!

(*Then suddenly forlornly tender.*)

Is it possible you can still love me, Ned?

DARRELL

(*Mournfully smiling.*)

I must, or I'd never act this fool way, would I!

NINA

(*Smiling back.*)

And I must love you.

(*Then seriously.*)

245

After all, I can never forget that Gordon is the child of your love, Ned.

DARRELL

(*Sadly.*)

You'd better forget that, for his sake and your own. Children have sure intuitions. He feels cheated of your love — by me. So he's concentrating his affections on Sam whose love he knows is secure, and withdrawing from you.

NINA

(*Frightened – angrily.*)

Don't be stupid, Ned! That isn't so at all! I hate you when you talk that way!

DARRELL

(*Cynically.*)

Hate me, exactly. As he does! That's what I'm advising you to do if you want to keep his love!

(*He smiles grimly.*)

NINA

(*Sharply.*)

If Gordon doesn't love you it's because you've never made the slightest attempt to be lovable to him! There's no earthly reason why he should like you, when you come right down to it, Ned! Take to-day, for instance. It's his birthday, but you'd forgotten, or didn't care! You never even brought him a present.

DARRELL

(With bitter sadness.)

I did bring him a present. It's out in the hall. I bought him a costly delicate one so he could get full satisfaction and yet not strain himself when he smashed it, as he's smashed every present of mine in the past! And I left it out in the hall, to be given to him after I've gone because, after all, he is my son and I'd prefer he didn't smash it before my eyes!

(Trying to mock his own emotion back – with savage bitterness.)

I'm selfish, you see! I don't want my son to be too happy at my expense, even on his birthday!

NINA

(Tormented by love and pity and remorse.)

Ned! For God's sake! How can you torture us like that! Oh, it's too dreadful – what I have done to you! Forgive me, Ned!

DARRELL

(His expression changing to one of pity for her – goes to her and puts his hand on her head – tenderly.)

I'm sorry.

(With remorseful tenderness.)

Dreadful, what you've done, Nina? Why, you've given me the only happiness I've ever known! And no matter what I may say or do in bitterness, I'm proud – and grateful, Nina!

NINA

(Looks up at him with deep tenderness and admiration.)

Dearest, it's wonderful of you to say that!

(She gets up and puts her hands on his shoulders and looks into his eyes — tenderly in a sort of pleading.)

Can't we be brave enough — for you to go away — now, on his note — sure of our love — with no ugly bitterness for once?

DARRELL

(Joyfully.)

Yes! I'll go — this minute if you wish!

NINA

(Playfully.)

Oh, you needn't go this minute! Wait and say good-bye to Sam. He'd be terribly hurt if you didn't.

(Then seriously.)

And will you promise to stay away two years — even if I call you back before then — and work this time, really work?

DARRELL

I'll try, Nina!

NINA

And then — surely come back to me!

DARRELL

(Smiling.)

Surely — again!

NINA

Then good-bye, dear!

(She kisses him.)

248

DARRELL

Again!

> (*He smiles and she smiles and they kiss again. Gordon appears in the doorway at rear and stands for a moment in a passion of jealousy and rage and grief, watching them.*)

GORDON

> (*Thinking with a strange tortured shame.*)
> I mustn't see her! . . . pretend I didn't see her! . . . mustn't never let her know I saw her! . . .
> (*He vanishes as silently as he had come.*)

NINA

> (*Suddenly moving away from Darrell, looking around her uneasily.*)

Ned, did you see – ? I had the queerest feeling just then that someone –

GORDON

> (*His voice sounds from the hall with a strained casualness.*)

Mother! Uncle Charlie's downstairs. Shall he come right up?

NINA

> (*Startled, her own voice straining to be casual.*)

Yes, dear – of course!

> (*Then worriedly.*)

His voice sounded funny. Did it to you? Do you suppose he – ?

DARRELL

(*With a wry smile.*)

It's possible. To be on the safe side, you'd better tell him you kissed me good-bye to get rid of me!

(*Then angrily.*)

So Marsden's here again! The damned old woman! I simply can't stand him any more, Nina! Why Gordon should take such a fancy to that old sissy is beyond me!

NINA

(*Suddenly struck – thinking.*)
Why, he's jealous of Gordon liking Charlie! . . .
(*Immediately all affectionate pity.*)
Then he must love Gordon a little! . . .
(*Letting her pity escape her.*)

Poor Ned!

(*She makes a movement toward him.*)

DARRELL

(*Startled and afraid she may have guessed something he doesn't acknowledge to himself.*)

What? why do you say that?

(*Then rudely defensive.*)

Don't be silly!

(*Resentfully.*)

You know well enough what I've always held against him! I wanted to put up all the money to back Sam when he started. I wanted to do it for Sam's sake – but especially for my child's sake. Why did Marsden absolutely insist on Sam letting him in equally? It isn't that I begrudge him the money he's made, but I know there was something queer in his mind and that he did it intentionally to spite me!

> (*From the hallway comes the sound of Marsden's voice and Gordon's greeting him vociferously as he lets him into the apartment. As Darrell listens his expression becomes furious again. He bursts out angrily.*)

You're letting that old ass spoil Gordon, you fool, you!

> (*Marsden comes in from the rear, smiling, immaculately dressed as usual. He looks hardly any older except that his hair is greyer and his tall figure more stooped. His expression and the general atmosphere he gives out are more nearly like those of Act One. If not happy, he is at least living in comparative peace with himself and his environment.*)

MARSDEN

> (*Comes straight to Nina.*)

Hallo, Nina Cara Nina! Congratulations on your son's birthday!

> (*He kisses her.*)

He's grown so much bigger and stronger in the two months since I've seen him.

> (*He turns and shakes hands with Darrell coldly – with a trace of a patronizing air.*)

Hallo, Darrell! Last time I was here you were leaving for the West Indies in a week, but I see you're still around.

DARRELL

> (*Furious – with a mocking air.*)

And here you are around again yourself! You're looking

comfortable these days, Marsden. I hope your sister is well.
It must be a great comfort, having her to take your mother's
place!

> (*Then with a harsh laugh.*)

Yes, we're two bad pennies, eh, Marsden? – counterfeits –
fakes – Sam's silent partners!

NINA

> (*Thinking irritably.*)
>
> Ned's getting hateful again! . . . Poor Charlie! . . . I
> won't have him insulted! . . . he's become such a comfort
> . . . he understands so much . . . without my having to
> tell him . . .
>
> (*Looking rebukingly at Darrell.*)

Ned is sailing this week, Charlie.

MARSDEN

> (*Thinking triumphantly.*)
>
> He's trying to insult me . . . I know all he means . . .
> but what do I care what he says . . . she's sending him
> away! . . . intentionally before me! . . . it means he's
> finished! . . .

DARRELL

> (*Thinking resentfully.*)
>
> Is she trying to humiliate me before him? . . . I'll teach
> her! . . .
>
> (*Then struggling with himself – remorsefully.*)
>
> No . . . not this time . . . I promised . . . no quarrel
> . . . remember . . .
>
> (*Acquiescing – with a pleasant nod to Marsden.*)

Yes, I'm going this week and I expect to be gone at least
two years this time – two years of hard work.

MARSDEN

(*Thinking with scornful pity.*)

His work! . . . what a pretence! . . . a scientific dilet-
tante! . . . could anything be more pitiable? . . . poor
chap! . . .

(*Perfunctorily.*)

Biology must be an interesting study. I wish I knew more
about it.

DARRELL

(*Stung yet amused by the other's tone – ironically.*)

Yes, so do I wish you did, Marsden! Then you might
write more about life and less about dear old ladies and devilish
bachelors! Why don't you write a novel about life some time,
Marsden?

(*He turns his back on Marsden with a glance of repulsion and walks to the window and stares out.*)

MARSDEN

(*Confusedly.*)

Yes – decidedly – but hardly in my line –

(*Thinking in anguish – picking up a magazine and
turning over the pages aimlessly.*)

That . . . is . . . true! . . . he's full of poison! . . . I've
never married the word to life! . . . I've been a timid
bachelor of Arts, not an artist! . . . my poor pleasant books!
. . . all is well! . . . is this well, the three of us? . . . Darrell
has become less and less her lover . . . Nina has turned
more and more to me . . . we have built up a secret life of
subtle sympathies and confidences . . . she has known I
have understood about her mere physical passion for Darrell
. . . what woman could be expected to love Sam passionately? . . . someday she'll confide all about Darrell to me
. . . now that he's finished . . . she knows that I love her

without my telling . . . **she** even knows the sort of love it
is. . . .

(*Passionately – thinking.*)

My love is finer than any she has known! . . . I do not
lust for her! . . . I would be content if our marriage should
be purely the placing of our ashes in the same tomb . . . our
urns side by side and touching one another . . . could the
others say as much, could they love so deeply? . . .

(*Then suddenly miserably self-contemptuous.*)

What! . . . platonic heroics at my age! . . . do I believe a
word of that? . . . look at her beautiful eyes! . . . wouldn't
I give anything in life to see them desire me? . . . and the
intimacy I'm boasting about, what more does it mean than
that I've been playing the dear old Charlie of her girlhood
again? . . .

(*Thinking in anguish.*)

Damned coward and weakling! . . .

NINA

(*Looking at him – pityingly – thinking.*)

What does he always want of me? . . . me? . . . I am
the only one who senses his deep hurt . . . I feel how life
has wounded him . . . is that partly my fault, too? . . I
have wounded everyone . . . poor Charlie, what can I do
for you? . . . if giving myself to you would bring you a
moment's happiness, could I? . . . the idea used to be revolting . . . now, nothing about love seems important
enough to be revolting . . . poor Charlie, he only thinks he
ought to desire me! . . . dear Charlie, what a perfect lover
he would make for one's old age! . . . what a perfect lover
when one was past passion! . . .

(*Then with sudden scornful revulsion.*)

These men make me sick! . . . I hate all three of them!
. . . they disgust me! . . . the wife and mistress in me has
been killed by them! . . . thank God, I am only a mother
now! . . . Gordon is my little man, my only man! . . .

(*Suddenly.*)

I've got a job for you, Charlie — make the salad dressing for lunch. You know, the one I'm so crazy about.

MARSDEN

(*Springs to his feet.*)

Right-o!

(*He puts his arm about her waist and they go out together laughingly, without a glance at Darrell.*)

DARRELL

(*Thinking dully.*)

I mustn't stay to lunch . . . ghost at my son's feast! . . . I better go now . . . why wait for Sam? . . . what is there to say to him I can say? . . . and there's nothing about him I want to see . . . he's as healthy as a pig . . . and as sane . . . I was afraid once his mother had lied to Nina . . . I went up-state and investigated . . . true, every word of it . . . his great-grandfather, his grandmother, his father, were all insane . . .

(*Moving uneasily.*)

Stop it! . . . time to go when those thoughts come . . . sail on Saturday . . . not come here again . . . Nina will soon be fighting Sam for my son's love! . . . I'm better out of that! . . . O Christ, what a mess it all is! . . .

GORDON

(*Appears in the doorway in rear. He carries a small, expensive model of a yacht with the sails set. He is in a terrific state of conflicting emotions, on the verge of tears yet stubbornly determined.*)

I got to do it! . . . Gosh, it's awful . . . this boat is so pretty . . . why did it have to come from him? . . . I can get Dad to buy me another boat . . . but now I love this one . . . but he kissed Mother . . . she kissed him . . .

(*He walks up defiantly and confronts Darrell, who turns to him in surprise.*)

Hey – Darrell – did you – ?

(*He stops chokingly.*)

DARRELL

(*Immediately realizing what is coming – thinking
with sombre anguish.*)

So this has to happen! . . . what I dreaded! . . . my fate
is merciless, it seems! . . .

(*With strained kindliness.*)

Did what?

GORDON

(*Growing hard – stammers angrily.*)

I found this – out in the hall. It can't be from anybody
else. Is this – your present?

DARRELL

(*Hard and defiant himself.*)

Yes.

GORDON

(*In a rage – tremblingly.*)

Then – here's what – I think of you!

(*Beginning to cry, he breaks off the mast, bowsprit,
breaks the mast in two, tears the rigging off and
throws the dismantled hull at Darrell's feet.*)

There! You can keep it!

DARRELL

(*His anger overcoming him for an instant.*)

You – you mean little devil, you! You don't get that from
me –

*(He has taken a threatening step forward. Gordon
stands white-faced, defying him. Darrell pulls
himself up short – then in a trembling voice of
deeply wounded affection.)*

You shouldn't have done that, son. What difference do I
make? It was never my boat. But it was your boat. You
should consider the boat, not me. Don't you like boats for
themselves? It was a beautiful little boat, I thought. That's
why I –

GORDON

(Sobbing miserably.)

It was awful pretty! I didn't want to do it!

*(He kneels down and gathers up the boat into his arms
again.)*

Honest I didn't. I love boats! But I hate you!

(This last with passionate intensity.)

DARRELL

(Dryly.)

So I've observed.

(Thinking with angry anguish.)
He hurts, damn him! . . .

GORDON

No, you don't know! More'n ever now! More'n ever!

(The secret escaping him.)

I saw you kissing Mother! I saw Mother, too!

DARRELL

(*Startled, but immediately forcing a smile.*)

But I was saying good-bye. We're old friends. You know that.

GORDON

You can't fool me! This was different!

(*Explosively.*)

It would serve you good and right – and Mother, too – if I was to tell Dad on you!

DARRELL

Why, I'm Sam's oldest friend. Don't make a little fool of yourself!

GORDON

You are not his friend. You've always been hanging around cheating him – hanging around Mother!

DARRELL

Rubbish! What do you mean cheating him?

GORDON

I don't know. But I know you aren't his friend. And some time I'm going to tell him I saw you –

DARRELL

(*With great seriousness now – deeply moved.*)

Listen! There are things a man of honour doesn't tell any-

258

one – not even his mother or father. You want to be a man of honour, don't you?

(*Intensely.*)

There are things we don't tell, you and I!

(*He has put his hand around Gordon's shoulder impulsively.*)

This is my son! . . . I love him! . . .

GORDON

(*Thinking – terribly torn.*)

Why do I like him now? . . . I like him awful! . . .

(*Crying.*)

We? – who d'you mean? – I've got honour! – more'n you! – you don't have to tell me! – I wasn't going to tell Dad, anyway, honest I wasn't! We? – what d'you mean, we? – I'm not like you! I don't want to be ever like you!

(*There is the sound of a door being flung open and shut and Evans' hearty voice.*)

EVANS

(*From the entrance hall.*)

Hallo, everybody!

DARRELL

(*Slapping Gordon on the back.*)

Buck up, son! Here he is! Hide that boat or he'll ask questions.

(*Gordon runs and hides the boat under the sofa. When Evans enters, Gordon is entirely composed and runs to him joyfully. Evans has grown stouter, his face is heavy now, he has*

259

*grown executive and used to command, he auto-
matically takes charge wherever he is. He does
not look his age except that his hair has grown
scanty and there is a perceptible bald spot on top.
He is expensively tailored.)*

EVANS

(Hugging Gordon to him – lovingly.)

How's the old son? How's the birthday coming along?

GORDON

Fine, Dad!

EVANS

Hallo, Ned! Isn't this kid of mine a whopper for his age,
though?

DARRELL

(Smiling strainedly.)

Yes.

(Writing – thinking.)

It hurts now! . . . to see my son his son! . . . I've had
enough! . . . get out! . . . any excuse! . . . I can 'phone
afterwards! . . . I'll yell out the whole business if I
stay! . . .

I was just going, Sam. I've got to step around and see a
fellow who lives near – biologist.

(He has gone to the door.)

EVANS

(Disappointedly.)

Then you won't be here for lunch?

260

STRANGE INTERLUDE

DARRELL

(*Thinking.*)

I'll yell the truth into your ears if I stay a second longer . . . you damned lunatic! . . .

Can't stay. Sorry. This is important. I'm sailing in a few days – lots to do – see you later, Sam. So long – Gordon.

(*He goes out with awkward haste.*)

GORDON

Good-bye – Uncle Ned.

(*Thinking confusedly.*)

Why did I call him that when I said I never would? . . . I know . . . must be because he said he's sailing and I'm glad . . .

EVANS

So long, Ned.

(*Thinking – good-naturedly superior.*)

Ned and his biology! . . . He takes his hobby pretty seriously! . . .

(*With satisfaction.*)

Well, he can afford to have hobbies now! . . . his investment with me has made him a pile. . . .

Where's Mother, son?

GORDON

Out in the kitchen with Uncle Charlie.

(*Thinking.*)

I hope he never comes back! . . . why did I like him then? . . . it was only for a second . . . I didn't really . . . I never could! . . . why does he always call me Gordon as if he hated to? . . .

261

EVANS

(*Sitting down at left.*)

I hope lunch is ready soon. I'm hungry as the devil, aren't you?

GORDON

(*Absent-mindedly.*)

Yes, Dad.

EVANS

Come over here and tell me about your birthday.

(*Gordon comes over. Evans pulls him up on his lap.*)

How'd you like your presents? What'd you get from Uncle Ned?

GORDON

(*Evasively.*)

They were all dandy.

(*Suddenly.*)

Why was I named Gordon?

EVANS

Oh, you know all about that — all about Gordon Shaw. I've told you time and again.

GORDON

You told me once he was Mother's beau — when she was a girl.

EVANS

(*Teasingly.*)

What do you know about beaux? You're growing up!

262

GORDON

Did Mother love him a lot?

EVANS

(*Embarrassedly.*)

I guess so.

GORDON

(*Thinking keenly.*)
That's why Darrell hates me being called Gordon . . .
he knows Mother loved Gordon better'n she does him . . .
now I know how to get back at him . . . I'll be just like
Gordon was and Mother'll love me better'n him! . . .

And then that Gordon was killed, wasn't he? Am I anything like him?

EVANS

I hope you are. If when you go to college you can play
football or row like Gordon did, I'll — I'll give you anything
you ask for! I mean that!

GORDON

(*Dreamily.*)

Tell me about him again, will you, Dad — about the time
he was stroking the crew and the fellow who was Number
Seven began to crack, and he couldn't see him but he felt him
cracking somehow, and he began talking back to him all the
time and sort of gave him his strength so that when the race
was over and they'd won Gordon fainted and the other fellow
didn't.

263

EVANS

(With a fond laugh.)

Why, you know it all by heart! What's the use of my telling you?

NINA

(Comes in from the rear while they are talking. She comes forward slowly.)
(Thinking resentfully.)
Does he love Sam more than he does me? . . . oh, no, he can't! . . . but he trusts him more! . . . he confides in him more! . . .

GORDON

Did you ever used to fight fellows, Dad?

EVANS

(Embarrassedly.)

Oh, a little – when I had to.

GORDON

Could you lick Darrell?

NINA

(Thinking frightenedly.)
Why does he ask that? . . .

EVANS

(Surprised.)

Your Uncle Ned? What for? We've always been friends.

GORDON

I mean, if you weren't friends, could you?

EVANS

(*Boastfully.*)

Oh, yes, I guess so. Ned was never as strong as I was.

NINA

(*Thinking contemptuously.*)
Ned is weak. . . .
(*Then apprehensively.*)
But you're getting too strong, Sam. . . .

GORDON

But Gordon could have licked you, couldn't he?

EVANS

You bet he could!

GORDON

(*Thinking.*)
She must have loved Gordon better'n Dad even! . . .

NINA

(*She comes forward to the chair at centre, forcing a smile.*)

What's all this talk about fighting? That's not nice. For heaven's sake, Sam, don't encourage him –

EVANS

(*Grinning.*)

Never mind the women, Gordon. You've got to know how to fight to get on in this world.

NINA

(Thinking pityingly.)
You poor booby! . . . how brave you are now! . . .
(Softly.)

Perhaps you're right, dear.

(Looking around.)

Has Ned gone?

GORDON

(Defiantly.)
Yes – and he's not coming back – and he's sailing soon !

NINA

(With a shudder.)
Why does he challenge me that way? . . and cling to
Sam? . . . he must have seen Ned and me . . . he doesn't
offer to come to my lap . . . he used to . . . Ned was right
. . . I've got to lie to him . . . get him back . . . here . . .
on my lap! . . .
(With a sneer – to Evans.)

I'm glad Ned's gone. I was afraid he was going to be on
our hands all day.

GORDON

(Eagerly, half getting down from his father's lap.)
You're glad – ?

(Then cautiously thinking.)
She's cheating . . . I saw her kiss him. . . .

NINA

Ned's getting to be an awful bore. He's so weak. He can't
get started on anything unless he's pushed.

GORDON

(*Moving a little nearer – searching her face – thinking.*)

She doesn't seem to like him so much . . but I saw her kiss him! . . .

EVANS

(*Surprised.*)

Oh, come now, Nina, aren't you being a little hard on Ned? It's true he's sort of lost his grip in a way, but he's our best friend.

GORDON

(*Moving away from his father again – resentfully – thinking.*)

What's Dad standing up for him to her for? . . .

NINA

(*Thinking triumphantly.*)

That's right, Sam . . just what I wanted you to say! . . .

(*Boredly.*)

Oh, I know he is, but he gets on my nerves hanging around all the time. Without being too rude, I urged him to get back to his work, and made him promise me he wouldn't return for two years. Finally he promised – and then he became silly and sentimental and asked me to kiss him good-bye for good luck! So I kissed him to get rid of him! The silly fool!

GORDON

(*Thinking – overjoyed.*)

Then! . . . that's why! . . . that's why! . . . and he'll be gone two years! . . . oh, I'm so glad! . . .

267

*(He goes to her and looks up into her face with shining
eyes.)*

Mother!

NINA

Dear!

*(She takes him up on her lap and hugs him in her
arms.)*

GORDON

(Kisses her.)

There!

(Triumphantly thinking.)

That makes up for his kiss! . . . That takes it off her
mouth. . . .

EVANS

(Grinning.)

Ned must be falling for you – in his old age!

(Then sentimentally.)

Poor guy! He's never married, that's the trouble. He's
lonely. I know how he feels. A fellow needs a little feminine
encouragement to help him keep his head up.

NINA

*(Snuggling Gordon's head against hers – laughing
teasingly.)*

I think your hard-headed Dad is getting mushy and silly!
What do you think, Gordon?

GORDON

(Laughing with her.)

Yes, he's mushy, Mother! He's silly!

(He kisses her and whispers.)

268

I'm going to be like Gordon Shaw, Mother!

(*She hugs him fiercely to her, triumphantly happy.*)

EVANS

(*Grinning.*)

You two are getting too hard-boiled for me.

(*He laughs. They all laugh happily together.*)

NINA

(*Suddenly overcome by a wave of conscience-stricken remorse and pity.*)

Oh, I am hard on Ned! . . . poor dear generous Ned!
. . . you told me to lie to your son against you . . . for my
sake . . . I'm not worthy of your love! . . . I'm low and
selfish! . . . but I do love you! . . . this is the son of our
love in my arms! . . . oh, Mother God, grant my prayer
that some day we may tell our son the truth and he may
love his father! . . .

GORDON

(*Sensing her thoughts, sits up in her lap and stares
into her face, while she guiltily avoids his eyes –
in fear and resentment.*)

(*Thinking.*)

She's thinking about that Darrell now! . . . I know! . . .
she likes him, too! . . . she can't fool me! . . . I saw her
kissing! . . . she didn't think he was a silly fool then! . . .
she was lying to Dad and me! . . .

(*He pushes off her lap and backs away from her.*)

NINA

(*Thinking frightenedly.*)

He read my thoughts! . . . I mustn't even think of Ned
when he's around! . . . poor Ned! . . . no, don't think of
him! . . .

> (*Leaning forward toward Gordon with her arms
> stretched out entreatingly but adopting a playful
> tone.*)

Why, Gordon, what's come over you? You jumped off my lap as though you'd sat on a tack!

> (*She forces a laugh.*)

GORDON

> (*His eyes on the floor – evasively.*)

I'm hungry. I want to see if lunch is nearly ready.

> (*He turns abruptly and runs out.*)

EVANS

> (*In a tone of superior manly understanding, kindly
> but laying down the law to womanly weakness.*)

He's sick of being babied, Nina. You forget he's getting to be a big boy. And we want him to grow up a real he-man and not an old lady like Charlie.

> (*Sagaciously.*)

That's what's made Charlie like he is, I'll bet. His mother never stopped babying him.

NINA

> (*Submissively – but with a look of bitter scorn at him.*)

Perhaps you're right, Sam.

EVANS

> (*Confidently.*)

I know I am!

STRANGE INTERLUDE

NINA

(*Thinking with a look of intense hatred.*)
Oh, Mother God, grant that I may some day tell this fool
the truth! . . .

(Curtain.)

ACT EIGHT

SCENE: *Late afternoon in late June, ten years later – the after-deck of the Evans' motor-cruiser anchored in the lane of yachts near the finish line at Poughkeepsie. The bow and amidship of the cruiser are off right, pointed upstream. The portside rail is in the rear, the curve of the stern at left, the rear of the cabin with broad windows and a door is at right. Two wicker chairs are at left and a chaise longue at right. A wicker table with another chair is at centre. The afterdeck is in cool shade, contrasted with the soft golden haze of late afternoon sunlight that glows on the river.*

Nina is sitting by the table at centre, Darrell in the chair farthest left, Marsden in the chaise longue at right. Evans is leaning over the rail just behind Nina, looking up the river through a pair of binoculars. Madeline Arnold is standing by his side.

Nina's hair has turned completely white. She is desperately trying to conceal the obvious inroads of time by an over-emphasis on make-up that defeats its end by drawing attention to what it would conceal. Her face is thin, her cheeks taut, her mouth drawn with forced smiling. There is little left of her face's charm except her eyes, which now seem larger and more deeply mysterious than ever. But she has kept her beautiful figure. It has the tragic effect of making her face seem older and more worn-out by contrast. Her general manner recalls instantly the Nina of Act Four, neurotic, passionately embittered and torn. She is dressed in a white yachting costume.

Darrell seems to have "thrown back" to the young doctor we had seen at the house of Nina's father in Act Two. He has again the air of the cool, detached scientist regarding himself and the people around him as interesting pheno- mena. In appearance, he is once more sharply defined, his face and body have grown lean and well-conditioned, the puffiness and jowls of the previous Act are gone. His skin is tanned almost black by his years in the tropics. His thick hair is iron-grey. He wears flannel pants, a blue coat, white buckskin shoes. He looks his fifty-one years, perhaps, but not a day more. Marsden has aged greatly. The stoop of his tall figure is accentuated, his hair has grown whitish. He is an older image of the Marsden of Act Five, who was so prostrated by his mother's death. Now it is his sister's death two months before that has plunged him into despair. His present grief, however, is more resigned to its fate than the old. He is dressed immaculately in black, as in Act Five.

Evans is simply Evans, his type logically developed by ten years of continued success and accumulating wealth, jovial and simple and good-natured as ever, but increasingly stub- born and self-opinionated. He has grown very stout. His jowly broad face has a heavy, flushed, apoplectic look. His head has grown quite bald on top. He is wearing a yachting cap, blue yachting coat, white flannel pants, buckskin shoes.

Madeline Arnold is a pretty girl of nineteen, with dark hair and eyes. Her skin is deeply tanned, her figure tall and athletic, reminding us of Nina's when we first saw her. Her personality is direct and frank. She gives the impres- sion of a person who always knows exactly what she is after and generally gets it, but is also generous and a good loser, a good sport who is popular with her own sex as well as sought after by men. She is dressed in a bright-coloured sports costume.

273

EVANS

(Nervous and excited – on pins and needles – lowering his binoculars impatiently.)

Can't see anything up there! There's a damned haze on the river!

(Handing the binoculars to Madeline.)

Here, Madeline. You've got young eyes.

MADELINE

(Eagerly.)

Thank you.

(She looks up the river through the glasses.)

NINA

(Thinking – bitterly.)

Young eyes! . . . they look into Gordon's eyes! . . . he sees love in her young eyes! . . . mine are old now! . . .

EVANS

(Pulling out his watch.)

Soon be time for the start.

(Comes forward – exasperatedly.)

Of course, the damned radio has to pick out this time to go dead! Brand new one I had installed especially for this race, too! Just my luck!

(Coming to Nina and putting his hand on her shoulder.)

Gosh, I'll bet Gordon's some keyed-up right at this moment, Nina!

MADELINE

(*Without lowering the glasses.*)

Poor kid! I'll bet he is!

NINA

(*Thinking with intense bitterness.*)

That tone in her voice! . . . her love already possesses
him! . . . my son! . . .

(*Vindictively.*)

But she won't! . . . as long as I live! . . .

(*Flatly.*)

Yes, he must be nervous.

EVANS

(*Taking his hand away, sharply.*)

I didn't mean nervous. He doesn't know what it is to have
nerves. Nothing's ever got him rattled yet.

(*This last with a resentful look down at her as he
moves back to the rail.*)

MADELINE

(*With the calm confidence of one who knows.*)

Yes, you can bank on Gordon never losing his nerve.

NINA

(*Coldly.*)

I'm quite aware my son isn't a weakling —

(*Meaningly, with a glance at Madeline.*)

even though he does do weak things sometimes.

275

MADELINE

(Without lowering the glasses from her eyes – thinking good-naturedly.)

Ouch! . . . that was meant for me! . . .

(Then hurt.)

Why does she dislike me so? . . . I've done my best, for Gordon's sake, to be nice to her. . . .

EVANS

(Looking back at Nina resentfully – thinking.)

Another nasty crack at Madeline! . . . Nina's certainly become the prize bum sport! . . . I thought once her change of life was over she'd be ashamed of her crazy jealousy . . . instead of that it's got worse . . . but I'm not going to let her come between Gordon and Madeline . . . he loves her and she loves him . . . and her folks have got money and position, too . . . and I like her a lot . . . and, by God, I'm going to see to it their marriage goes through on schedule, no matter how much Nina kicks up! . . .

DARRELL

(Keenly observant – thinking.)

Nina hates this young lady . . . of course! . . . Gordon's girl . . . she'll smash their engagement if she can . . . as she did mine once . . . once! . . . thank God my slavery is over! . . . how did she know I was back in town? . . . I wasn't going to see her again . . . but her invitation was so imploring . . . my duty to Gordon, she wrote . . . what duty? . . . pretty late in the day! . . . that's better left dead, too! . . .

EVANS

(Looking at his watch again.)

They ought to be lined up at the start any minute now

(*Pounding his fist on the rail – letting his pent-up feelings explode.*)

Come on, Gordon!

NINA

(*Startled – with nervous irritation.*)

Sam! I told you I have a splitting headache!

(*Thinking intensely.*)

You vulgar boor! . . . Gordon's engagement to her is all your fault! . . .

EVANS

(*Resentfully.*)

I'm sorry. Why don't you take some aspirin?

(*Thinking irritably.*)

Nina in the dumps! . . . Charlie in mourning! . . . what a pair of killjoys! . . . I wanted to bring Gordon and his friends on board to celebrate . . . no chance! . . . have to take Madeline . . . stage a party in New York . . . leave this outfit flat . . . Nina'll be sore as the devil, but she'll have to like it . . .

DARRELL

(*Examining Nina critically – thinking.*)

She's got into a fine neurotic state . . . reminds me of when I first knew her . . .

(*Then exultantly.*)

Thank God, I can watch her objectively again . . . these last three years away have finally done it . . . complete cure! . . .

(*Then remorsefully.*)

Poor Nina! . . . we're all deserting her . . .

(*Then glancing at Marsden – with a trace of a sneer.*)

Even Marsden seems to have left her for the dead! . .

STRANGE INTERLUDE

MARSDEN

(*Vaguely irritated – thinking.*)

What am I doing here? . . . what do I care about this stupid race? . . . why did I let Nina bully me into coming? . . . I ought to be alone . . . with my memories of dear Jane . . . it will be two months on Saturday since she died . . .

(*His lips tremble, tears come to his eyes.*)

MADELINE

(*With an impatient sigh, lowering the glasses.*)

It's no use, Mr. Evans, I can't see a thing.

EVANS

(*With angry disgust.*)

If only that damned radio was working!

NINA

(*Exasperatedly.*)

For heaven's sake, stop swearing so much!

EVANS

(*Hurt – indignantly.*)

What about it if I am excited? Seems to me you could show a little more interest without it hurting you, when it's Gordon's last race, his last appearance on a 'varsity!

(*He turns away from her.*)

MADELINE

(*Thinking.*)

He's right . . . she's acting rotten . . . if I were Gordon's mother, I certainly wouldn't . . .

278

EVANS

(*Turning back to Nina – resentfully.*)

You used to cheer loud enough for Gordon Shaw! And our Gordon's got him beat a mile, as an oarsman, at least!

(*Turning to Darrell.*)

And that isn't father stuff either, Ned! All the experts say so!

DARRELL

(*Cynically.*)

Oh, come on, Sam! Surely no one could ever touch Shaw in anything!

(*He glances at Nina with a sneer.*)
(*Immediately angry at himself.*)
What an idiot! . . . that popped out of me! . . . old habit! . . . For years I haven't loved her! . . .

NINA

(*Thinking indifferently.*)
Ned still feels jealous . . . that no longer pleases me . . . I don't feel anything . . . except that I must get him to help me.

(*She turns to Darrell bitterly.*)

Sam said "our" Gordon. He means his. Gordon's become so like Sam, Ned, you won't recognize him!

MADELINE

(*Thinking indignantly.*)
She's crazy! . . . he's nothing like his father! . . . he's so strong and handsome! . . .

279

EVANS

(*Good-naturedly, with a trace of pride.*)

You flatter me, Nina. I wish I thought that. But he isn't a bit like me, luckily for him. He's the living image of Gordon Shaw at his best.

MADELINE

(*Thinking.*)

Shaw . . . I've seen his picture in the gym . . . my Gordon is better looking . . . he once told me Shaw was an old beau of his mother's . . . they say she was beautiful once . . .

NINA

(*Shaking her head – scornfully.*)

Don't be modest, Sam. Gordon *is* you. He may be a fine athlete like Gordon Shaw, because you've held that out to him as your ideal, but there the resemblance ceases. He isn't really like him at all, not the slightest bit!

EVANS

(*Restraining his anger with difficulty – thinking.*)

I'm getting sick of this! . . . she's carrying her jealousy too far! . . .

(*Suddenly exploding, pounds his fist on the rail.*)

Damn it, Nina, if you had any feeling you couldn't – right at the moment when he's probably getting into the shell –

(*He stops, trying to control himself, panting, his face red.*)

NINA

(*Staring at him with repulsion – with cool disdain.*)

I didn't say anything so dire, did I – merely that Gordon resembles you in character.

(*With malice.*)

Don't get so excited. It's bad for your high blood pressure. Ask Ned if it isn't.

(*Intensely – thinking.*)
If he'd only die! . . .
(*Thinking – immediately.*)
Oh, I don't mean that . . . I mustn't . . .

DARRELL

(*Thinking keenly.*)
There's a death wish . . . things have gone pretty far . . . Sam does look as if he might have a bad pressure . . . what hope that would have given me at one time! . . . no more, thank God! . . .
(*In a joking tone.*)

Oh, I guess Sam's all right, Nina.

EVANS

(*Gruffly.*)

I never felt better.

(*He jerks out his watch again.*)

Time for the start. Come on in the cabin, Ned, and have a drink. We'll see if McCabe's getting the damned radio fixed.

(*Passing by Marsden he claps him on the shoulder exasperatedly.*)

Come on, Charlie! Snap out of it!

MARSDEN

(*Startled out of his trance – bewilderedly.*)

Eh? – what is it? – are they coming?

EVANS

(Recovering his good nature – with a grin, taking his arm.)

You're coming to have a drink. You need about ten, I think, to get you in the right spirit to see the finish!

(To Darrell, who has got up but is still standing by his chair.)

Come on, Ned.

NINA

(Quickly.)

No, leave Ned with me. I want to talk to him. Take Madeline – and Charlie.

MARSDEN

(Looking at her appealingly.)

But I'm perfectly contented sitting –

(Then after a look in her eyes – thinking.)

She wants to be alone with Darrell . . . all right . . . doesn't matter now . . . their love is dead . . . but there's still some secret between them she's never told me . . . never mind . . . she'll tell me some time . . . I'm all she will have left . . . soon. . . .

(Then stricken with guilt.)

Poor dear Jane! . . . how can I think of anyone but you! . . . God, I'm contemptible! . . . I'll get drunk with that fool! . . . that's all I'm good for! . . .

MADELINE

(Thinking resentfully.)

She takes a fine do-this-little-girl tone toward me! . . . I'll give in to her now . . . but once I'm married! . . .

STRANGE INTERLUDE

Come on then, Madeline. We'll give you a small one.

(Impatiently.)

Charlie! Head up!

MARSDEN

(With hectic joviality.)

I hope it's strong poison!

EVANS

(Laughing.)

That's the spirit! We'll make a sport out of you yet!

MADELINE

(Laughing, goes and takes Marsden's arm.)

I'll see you get home safe, Mr. Marsden!

> *(They go into the cabin, Evans following them. Nina and Darrell turn and look at each other wonderingly, inquisitively, for a long moment. Darrell remains standing and seems to be a little uneasy.)*

DARRELL

(Thinking with melancholy interest.)

And now? . . . what? . . . I can look into her eyes . . . strange eyes that will never grow old . . . without desire or jealousy or bitterness . . . was she ever my mistress? . . . can she be the mother of my child? . . . is there such a person as my son? . . . I can't think of these things as real any more . . . they must have happened in another life. . . .

NINA

(Thinking sadly.)

My old lover . . . how well and young he looks! . . . now we no longer love each other at all . . . our account with God the Father is settled . . . afternoons of happiness paid for with years of pain . . . love, passion, ecstasy . . . in what a far-off life were they alive! . . . the only living life is in the past and future . . . the present is an interlude . . . strange interlude in which we call on past and future to bear witness we are living! . . .

(With a sad smile.)

Sit down, Ned. When I heard you were back I wrote you because I need a friend. It has been so long since we loved each other we can now be friends again. Don't you feel that?

DARRELL

(Gratefully.)

Yes. I do.

(He sits down in one of the chairs at left, drawing it up closer to her.)

(Thinking cautiously.)

I want to be her friend . . . but I will never . . .

NINA

(Thinking cautiously.)

I must keep very cool and sensible or he won't help me. . . .

(With a friendly smile.)

I haven't seen you look so young and handsome since I first knew you. Tell me your secret.

(Bitterly.)

I need it! I'm old! Look at me! And I was actually looking forward to being old! I thought it would mean peace. I've been sadly disillusioned!

(*Then forcing a smile.*)

So tell me what fountain of youth you've found.

DARRELL

(*Proudly.*)

That's easy. Work! I've become as interested in biology as I once was in medicine. And not selfishly interested, that's the difference. There's no chance of my becoming a famous biologist and I know it. I'm very much a worker in the ranks. But our Station is a "huge success," as Sam would say. We've made some damned important discoveries. I say "we." I really mean Preston. You may remember I used to write you about him with enthusiasm. He's justified it. He *is* making his name world-famous. He's what I might have been – I did have the brains, Nina! – if I'd had more guts and less vanity, if I'd hewn to the line!

(*Then forcing a smile.*)

But I'm not lamenting. I've found myself in helping him. In that way I feel I've paid my debt – that his work is partly my work. And he acknowledges it. He possesses the rare virtue of gratitude.

(*With proud affection.*)

He's a fine boy, Nina! I suppose I should say man now he's in his thirties.

NINA

(*Thinking with bitter sorrow.*)

So, Ned . . . you remember our love . . with bitterness! . . . as a stupid mistake! . . . the proof of a gutless vanity that ruined your career! . . . oh! . . .

285

(*Then controlling herself – thinking cynically.*)

Well, after all, how do I remember our love? . . . with no emotion at all, not even bitterness! . . .

(*Then with sudden alarm.*)

He's forgotten Gordon for this Preston! . . .

(*Thinking desperately.*)

I must make him remember Gordon is his child or I can never persuade him to help me! . . .

(*Reproachfully.*)

So you have found a son while I was losing mine – who is yours, too!

DARRELL

(*Struck by this – impersonally interested.*)

That's never occurred to me, but now I think of it –

(*Smiling.*)

Yes, perhaps unconsciously Preston is a compensating substitute. Well, it's done both of us good and hasn't harmed anyone.

NINA

(*With bitter emphasis.*)

Except your real son – and me – but we don't count, I suppose!

DARRELL

(*Coolly.*)

Harmed Gordon? How? He's all right, isn't he?

(*With a sneer.*)

I should say from all I've been hearing that he was your ideal of college hero – like his never-to-be-forgotten namesake!

NINA

(*Thinking resentfully.*)
He's sneering at his own son! . . .

(*Then trying to be calculating.*)
But I mustn't get angry . . . I must make him **help**
me. . .

(*Speaking with gentle reproach.*)

And am I the ideal of a happy mother, Ned?

DARRELL

(*Immediately moved by pity and ashamed of himself.*)

Forgive me, Nina. I haven't quite buried all my bitterness,
I'm afraid.

(*Gently.*)

I'm sorry you're unhappy, Nina.

NINA

(*Thinking with satisfaction.*)
He means that . . he still does care a little . . . if only
it's enough to . . .

(*Speaking sadly.*)

I've lost my son, Ned! Sam has made him all his. And it
was done so gradually that, although I realized what was
happening, there was never any way I could interfere. What
Sam advised seemed always the best thing for Gordon's future.
And it was always what Gordon himself wanted, to escape
from me to boarding school and then to college, to become
Sam's athletic hero —

DARRELL

(*Impatiently.*)

Oh, come now, Nina, you know you've always longed for
him to be like Gordon Shaw!

STRANGE INTERLUDE

NINA

(*Bursting out in spite of herself – violently*.)

He's not like Gordon! He's forgotten me for that – !

(*Trying to be more reasonable*.)

What do I care whether he's an athlete or not? It's such nonsense, all this fuss! I'm not the slightest bit interested in this race to-day, for example! I wouldn't care if he came in last!

(*Stopping herself – thinking frightenedly*.)
Oh, if he should ever guess I said that! . . .

DARRELL

(*Thinking keenly*.)
Hallo! . . . she said that as if she'd like to see him come last! . . why? . . .
(*Then vindictively*.)
Well, so would I! . . . it's time these Gordons took a good licking from life! . . .

MADELINE

(*Suddenly appears in the doorway of the cabin, her face flushed with excitement*.)

They're off! Mr. Evans is getting something – it's terribly faint, but – Navy and Washington are leading – Gordon's third!

(*She disappears again in the cabin*.)

NINA

(*Looking after her with hatred*.)
Her Gordon! . . . she is so sure! . . . how I've come to detest her pretty face! . . .

288

DARRELL

(*Thinking with a sneer.*)
"Gordon's third"! . . . you might think there was no one
else pulling the shell! . . . what idiots women make of themselves about these Gordons! . . . she's pretty, that Madeline! . . . she's got a figure like Nina's when I first loved
her . . . those afternoons . . . age is beginning to tell on
Nina's face . . . but she's kept her wonderful body! . . .
(*With a trace of malice – dryly.*)

There's a young lady who seems to care a lot whether
Gordon comes in last or not!

NINA

(*Trying to be sorrowful and appealing.*)
Yes. Gordon is hers now, Ned.
(*But she cannot bear this thought – vindictively.*)

That is, they're engaged. But, of course, that doesn't neces-
sarily mean – Can you imagine him throwing himself away
on a little fool like that? I simply can't believe he really loves
her! Why, she's hardly even pretty and she's deadly stupid. I
thought he was only flirting with her – or merely indulging in
a passing physical affair.

(*She winces.*)

At his age, one has to expect – even a mother must face
nature. But for Gordon to take her seriously, and propose
marriage – it's too idiotic for words!

DARRELL

(*Thinking cynically.*)
Oh, so you'll compromise on his sleeping with her . . . if
you have to . . . but she must have no real claim to dispute

K   289

your ownership, eh? . . . you'd like to make her the same sort of convenient slave for him that I was for you! . . .
(*Resentfully.*)

I can't agree with you. I find her quite charming. It seems to me if I were in Gordon's shoes I'd do exactly what he has done.

(*In confusion – thinking bitterly.*)
In Gordon's shoes! . . . I always was in Gordon Shaw's shoes! . . . and why am I taking this young Gordon's part? . . . what is he to me, for God's sake? . . .

NINA

(*Unheedingly.*)

If he marries her, it means he'll forget me! He'll forget me as completely as Sam forgot his mother! She'll keep him away from me! Oh, I know what wives can do! She'll use her body until she persuades him to forget me! My son, Ned! And your son, too!

(*She suddenly gets up and goes to him and takes one of his hands in both of hers.*)

The son of our old love, Ned!

DARRELL

(*Thinking with a strange shudder of mingled attraction and fear as she touches him.*)
Our love . . . old love . . . old touch of her flesh . . . we're old . . . it's silly and indecent . . . does she think she still can own me? . . .

NINA

(*In the tone a mother takes in speaking to her husband about their boy.*)

You'll have to give Gordon a good talking to, Ned.

DARRELL

(*Still more disturbed – thinking.*)

Old . . . but she's kept her wonderful body . . . how many years since? . . . she has the same strange influence over me . . . touch of her flesh . . . it's dangerous . . . bosh, I'm only humouring her as a friend . . . as her doctor . . . and why shouldn't I have a talk with Gordon? . . . a father owes something to his son . . . he ought to advise him. . . .

(*Then alarmed.*)

But I was never going to meddle again . . .

(*Sternly.*)

I swore I'd never again meddle with human lives, Nina!

NINA

(*Unheedingly.*)

You must keep him from ruining his life.

DARRELL

(*Doggedly – struggling with himself.*)

I won't touch a life that has more than one cell!

(*Harshly.*)

And I wouldn't help you in this, anyway! You've got to give up owning people, meddling in their lives as if you were God and had created them!

NINA

(*Strangely forlorn.*)

I don't know what you mean, Ned. Gordon is my son, isn't he?

DARRELL

(*With a sudden strange violence.*)

And mine! Mine, too!

(*He stops himself.*)
(*Thinking.*)
Shut up, you fool! . . . is that the way to humour her?
. . .

NINA

(*With strange quiet.*)

I think I still love you a little, Ned.

DARRELL

(*In her tone.*)

And I still love you a little, Nina.

(*Then sternly.*)

But I will not meddle in your life again!

(*With a harsh laugh.*)

And you've meddled enough with human love, old lady!
Your time for that is over! I'll send you a couple of million
cells you can torture without harming yourself!

(*Regaining control – shamefacedly.*)

Nina! Please forgive me!

NINA

(*Starts as if out of a dream – anxiously.*)

What were you saying, Ned?

(*She lets go of his hand and goes back to her chair.*)

292

DARRELL

(Dully.)

Nothing.

NINA

(Strangely.)

We were talking about Sam, weren't we? How do you
think he looks?

DARRELL

(Confusedly casual.)

Fine. A bit too fat, of course. He looks as though his
blood pressure might be higher than it ought to be. But that's
not unusual in persons of his build and age. It's nothing to
hope – I meant, to worry over!

(Then violently.)

God damn it, why did you make me say hope?

NINA

(Calmly.)

It may have been in your mind, too, mayn't it?

DARRELL

No! I've nothing against Sam. I've always been his best
friend. He owes his happiness to me.

NINA

(Strangely.)

There are so many curious reasons we dare not think about
for thinking things!

DARRELL

(*Rudely.*)

Thinking doesn't matter a damn! Life is something in one cell that doesn't need to think!

NINA

(*Strangely.*)

I know! God the Mother!

DARRELL

(*Excitedly.*)

And all the rest is gutless egotism! But to hell with it! What I started to say was, what possible reason could I have for hoping for Sam's death?

NINA

(*Strangely.*)

We're always desiring death for ourselves or others, aren't we – while we while away our lives with the old surface ritual of coveting our neighbour's ass?

DARRELL

(*Frightenedly.*)

You're talking like the old Nina now – when I first loved you. Please don't! It isn't decent – at our age!

(*Thinking in terror.*)
   The old Nina! . . . am I the old Ned? . . . then that means? . . . but we must not meddle in each other's lives again! . . .

294

NINA

(Strangely.)

I am the old Nina! And this time I will not let my Gordon go from me for ever!

EVANS

(Appears in the doorway of the cabin – excited and irritated.)

Madeline's listening in now. It went dead on me.

(Raising the binoculars as he goes to the rail, he looks up the river.)

Last I got, Gordon third, Navy and Washington leading. They're the ones to fear, he said – Navy especially.

(Putting down the glasses – with a groan.)

Damned haze! My eyes are getting old.

(Then suddenly with a grin.)

You ought to see Charlie! He started throwing Scotch into him as if he were drinking against time. I had to take the bottle away from him. It's hit him an awful wallop.

(Then looking from one to the other – resentfully.)

What's the matter with you two? There's a race going on, don't you know it? And you sit like dead clams!

DARRELL

(Placatingly.)

I thought someone'd better stay out here and let you know when they get in sight.

EVANS

(Relieved.)

Oh, sure, that's right! Here, take the glasses. You always had good eyes.

> *(Darrell gets up and takes the glasses and goes to the rail and begins adjusting them.)*

DARRELL

Which crew was it you said Gordon feared the most?

EVANS

(Has gone back to the cabin doorway.)

Navy.

(Then proudly.)

Oh, he'll beat them! But it'll be damn close. I'll see if Madeline's getting —

> *(He goes into the cabin.)*

DARRELL

(Looking up the river – with vindictive bitterness – thinking.)

Come on, Navy! . . .

NINA

(Thinking bitterly.)

Madeline's Gordon! . . . Sam's Gordon! . . . the thanks I get for saving Sam at the sacrifice of my own happiness! . . . I won't have it! . . . what do I care what happens to Sam now? . . . I hate him! . . . I'll tell him Gordon isn't his child! . . . and threaten to tell Gordon, too, unless! . . . he'll be in deadly fear of that! . . . he'll soon find some excuse to break their engagement! . . . he can! . . . he has

296

the strangest influence over Gordon! . . . but Ned **must**
back me up or Sam won't believe me! . . . Ned must
tell him, too! . . . but will Ned? . . . he'll be afraid of
the insanity! . . . I must make him believe Sam's in no
danger . . .

> (*Intensely.*)

Listen, Ned, I'm absolutely sure, from things she wrote me
before she died, that Sam's mother must have been deliberately lying to me about the insanity that time. She was jealous
because Sam loved me and she simply wanted to be revenged,
I'm sure.

DARRELL

> (*Without lowering glasses – dryly.*)

No. She told you the truth. I never mentioned it, but I
went up there once and made a thorough investigation of his
family.

NINA

> (*With resentful disappointment.*)

Oh – I suppose you wanted to make sure so you could hope
he'd go insane?

DARRELL

> (*Simply.*)

I needed to be able to hope that, then. I loved you horribly
at that time, Nina – horribly!

NINA

> (*Putting her hands on his arm.*)

And you don't – any more, Ned?

> (*Thinking intensely.*)
> Oh, I must make him love me **again** . . . enough to make
> him tell Sam! . . .

297

DARRELL

(*Thinking strangely – struggling with himself.*)
She'd like to own me again . . . I wish she wouldn't touch me . . . what is this tie of old happiness between our flesh? . . .
(*Harshly – weakly struggling to shake off her hands, without lowering the glasses.*)

I won't meddle again with human lives, I told you!

NINA

(*Unheeding, clinging to him.*)

And I loved you horribly! I still do love you, Ned! I used to hope he'd go insane myself because I loved you so! But look at Sam! He's sane as a pig! There's absolutely no danger now!

DARRELL

(*Thinking – alarmed.*)
What is she after now . . . what does she want me for? . . .
(*Stiffly.*)

I'm no longer a doctor, but I should say he's a healthy miss of Nature's. It's a thousand to one against it at this late day.

NINA

(*With sudden fierce intensity.*)

Then it's time to tell him the truth, isn't it? We've suffered all our lives for his sake! We've made him rich and happy! It's time he gave us back our son!

DARRELL

(Thinking.)
Aha . . . so that's it! . . . tell Sam the truth? . . . at
last! . . . by God, I'd like to tell him, at that! . . .
(With a sneer.)

Our son? You mean yours, my dear! Kindly count me
out of any further meddling with ·

NINA

(Unruffledly – obsessed.)

But Sam won't believe me if I'm the only one to tell him!
He'll think I'm lying for spite, that it's only my crazy
jealousy! He'll ask you! You've got to tell him too, Ned!

DARRELL

(Thinking.)
I'd like to see his face when I told him this famous oarsman isn't his son but mine! . . . that might pay me back a
little for all he's taken from me! . . .
(Harshly.)

I've stopped meddling in Sam's life, I tell you!

NINA

(Insistently.)

Think of what Sam has made us go through, of how he's
made us suffer! You've got to tell him! You still love me a
little, don't you, Ned? You must when you remember the
happiness we've known in each other's arms! You were the
only happiness I've ever known in life!

DARRELL

(*Struggling weakly – thinking.*)
She lies! . . . there was her old lover, Gordon! . . he
was always first! . . . then her son, Gordon! . . .
(*With desperate rancour – thinking.*)
Come on, Navy! . . . beat her Gordons for me! . . .

NINA

(*Intensely.*)

Oh, if I'd only gone away with you that time when you
came back from Europe! How happy we would have been,
dear! How our boy would have loved you – if it hadn't been
for Sam!

DARRELL

(*Thinking – weakly.*)
Yes, if it hadn't been for Sam I would have been happy!
. . . I would have been the world's greatest neurologist!
. . . my boy would have loved me and I'd have loved
him! . . .

NINA

(*With a crowning intensity to break down his last
resistance.*)

You must tell him, Ned! For my sake! Because I love
you! Because you remember our afternoons – our mad happiness! Because you love me!

DARRELL

(*Beaten – dazedly.*)

Yes – what must I do? – meddle again?

(*The noise of Madeline's excited voice cheering and
clapping her hands, of Marsden's voice yelling
drunkenly, of Evans', all shouting, "Gordon!*

300

Gordon! Come on, Gordon!" comes from the
cabin. Marsden appears swaying in the cabin
doorway yelling, "Gordon!" He is hectically
tipsy. Darrell gives a violent shudder as if he
were coming out of a nightmare and pushes Nina
away from him.)

DARRELL

(*Thinking – dazedly still, but in a tone of relief.*)
Marsden again! . . . thank God! . . . he's saved me! . . .
from her! . . . and her Gordons! . . .
(*Turning on her triumphantly.*)

No, Nina – sorry – but I can't help you. I told you I'd
never meddle again with human lives!

(*More and more confidently.*)

Besides, I'm quite sure Gordon isn't my son, if the real
deep core of the truth were known! I was only a body to you.
Your first Gordon used to come back to life. I was never
more to you than a substitute for your dead lover! Gordon is
really Gordon's son! So you see I'd be telling Sam a lie if I
boasted that I – And I'm a man of honour! I've proved that,
at least!

(*He raises his glasses and looks up the river.*)
(*Thinking exultantly.*)
I'm free! . . . I've beaten her at last! . . . now come on,
Navy! . . . you've got to beat her Gordons for me! . . .

NINA

(*After staring at him for a moment – walking away*
from him – thinking with a dull fatalism.)
I've lost him . . . he'll never tell Sam now . . . is what
he said right? . . . is Gordon Gordon's? . . . oh, I hope so!
. . . oh, dear, dead Gordon, help me to get back your son!
. . . I must find some way. . . .
(*She sits down again.*)

301

MARSDEN

(Who has been staring at them with a foolish grin.)

Hallo, you two! Why do you look so guilty? You don't love each other any more! It's all nonsense! I don't feel the slightest twinge of jealousy. That's proof enough, isn't it?

(Then blandly apologetic.)

Pardon me if I sound a bit pipped – a good bit! Sam said ten and then took the bottle away when I'd had only five! But it's enough! I've forgotten sorrow! There's nothing in life worth grieving about, I assure you, Nina! And I've got interested in this race now.

(He sings raucously.)

"Oh, we'll row, row, row, right down the river! And we'll row, row, row –" Remember that old tune – when you were a little girl, Nina? Oh, I'm forgetting Sam said to tell you Gordon was on even terms with the leaders! A gallant spurt did it! Touch and go now! I don't care who wins – as long as it isn't Gordon! I don't like him since he's grown up! He thinks I'm an old woman!

(Sings.)

"Row, row, row." The field against Gordon!

DARRELL

(Hectically.)

Right!

(He looks through the glasses – excitedly.)

I see a flashing in the water way up there! Must be their oars! They're coming! I'll tell Sam!

(He hurries into the cabin.)

NINA

(*Thinking dully.*)
He'll tell Sam . . . no, he doesn't mean that . . . I must
find some other way . . .

MARSDEN

(*Walks a bit uncertainly to Nina's chair.*)

Gordon really should get beaten to-day – for the good of
his soul, Nina. That Madeline is pretty, isn't she? These
Gordons are too infernally lucky – while we others –

(*He almost starts to blubber – angrily.*)

we others have got to beat him to-day!

(*He slumps clumsily down to a sitting position on the
deck by her chair and takes her hand and pats
it.*)

There, there, Nina Cara Nina! Don't worry your pretty
head! It will all come out all right! We'll only have a little
while longer to wait and then you and I'll be quietly married!

(*Thinking frightenedly.*)
The devil! . . . what am I saying? . . . I'm drunk! . . .
all right, all the better! . . . I've wanted all my life to tell
her! . . .

Of course, I realize you've got a husband at present, but
never mind, I can wait. I've waited a lifetime already; but
for a long while now I've had a keen psychic intuition that
I wasn't born to die before –

(*Evans and Madeline and Darrell come rushing out
of the cabin. They all have binoculars. They
run to the rail and train their glasses up the
river.*)

303

MADELINE

(*Excitedly.*)

I see them!

(*Grabbing his arm and pointing.*)

Look, Mr. Evans – there – don't you see?

EVANS

(*Excitedly.*)

No – not yet – Yes! Now I see them!

(*Pounding on the rail.*)

Come on, Gordon boy!

MADELINE

Come on, Gordon!

(*The whistles and sirens from the yachts up the river begin to be heard. This grows momentarily louder as one after another other yachts join in the chorus as the crews approach nearer and nearer until toward the close of the scene there is a perfect pandemonium of sound.*)

NINA

(*With bitter hatred – thinking.*)

How I hate her! . . .

(*Then suddenly with a deadly calculation – thinking.*)

Why not tell her? . . . as Sam's mother told me . . . of the insanity? . . . she thinks Gordon is Sam's son. . . .

(*With a deadly smile of triumph.*)

That will be poetic justice! . . . that will solve everything! . . . she won't marry him! . . . he will turn to me for comfort! . . . but I must plan it out carefully! . . .

304

MARSDEN

(Driven on – extravagantly.)

Listen, Nina! After we're married I'm going to write a novel – my first real novel! All the twenty odd books I've written have been long-winded fairy tales for grown-ups – about dear old ladies and witty, cynical bachelors and quaint characters with dialects, and married folk who always admire and respect each other, and lovers who avoid love in hushed whispers! That's what I've been, Nina – a hush-hush whisperer of lies! Now I'm going to give an honest healthy yell – turn on the sun into the shadows of lies – shout "This is life and this is sex, and here are passion and hatred and regret and joy and pain and ecstasy, and these are men and women and sons and daughters whose hearts are weak and strong, whose blood is blood and not a soothing syrup!" Oh, I can do it, Nina! I can write the truth! I've seen it in you, your father, my mother, sister, Gordon, Sam, Darrell, and myself. I'll write the book of us! But here I am talking while my last chapters are in the making – right here and now –

(Hurriedly.)

You'll excuse me, won't you, Nina? I must watch – my duty as an artist!

> *(He scrambles to his feet and peers about him with a hectic eagerness. Nina pays no attention to him.)*

EVANS

(Exasperatedly, taking down his glasses.)

You can't tell a damn thing – which is which or who's ahead – I'm going to listen in again.

(He hurries into the cabin.)

NINA

(With a smile of cruel triumph – thinking.)
I can tell her . . . confidentially . . . I can pretend I'm
forced to tell her . . . as Sam's mother did with me . . .
because I feel it's due to her happiness and Gordon's . . . it
will explain my objection to the engagement . . . oh, it
can't help succeeding . . . my Gordon will come back! . . .
I'll see he never gets away again! . . .

(She calls.)

Madeline!

MARSDEN

(Thinking.)
Why is she calling Madeline? . . . I must watch all this
carefully! . . .

EVANS

(Comes rushing out in wild alarm.)

Bad news! Navy has drawn ahead – half a length – looks
like Navy's race, he said –

(Then violently.)

But what does he know, that damn fool announcer – some
poor boob – !

MADELINE

(Excitedly.)

He doesn't know Gordon! He's always best when he's
pushed to the limit!

NINA

(She calls more sharply.)

Madeline!

DARRELL

(*Turns around to stare at her – thinking.*)
Why is she calling Madeline? . . . she's bound she'll
meddle in their lives . . . I've got to watch her . . . well,
let's see. . . .

(*He touches Madeline on the shoulder.*)

Mrs. Evans is calling you, Miss Arnold.

MADELINE

(*Impatiently.*)

Yes, Mrs. Evans. But they're getting closer. Why don't
you come and watch?

NINA

(*Not heeding – impressively.*)

There's something I must tell you.

MADELINE

(*In hopeless irritation.*)

But – Oh, all right!

(*She hurries over to her, glancing eagerly over her
shoulder toward the river.*)

Yes, Mrs. Evans?

DARRELL

(*Moves from the rail toward them – thinking keenly.*)
I must watch this . . . she's in a desperate meddling
mood! . . .

NINA

(*Impressively.*)

First, give me your word of honour that you'll never reveal

a word of what I'm going to tell you to a living soul – above all not to Gordon!

MADELINE

(*Looking at her in amazement – soothingly.*)

Couldn't you tell me later, Mrs. Evans – after the race?

NINA

(*Sternly – grabbing her by the wrist.*)

No, now! Do you promise?

MADELINE

(*With helpless annoyance.*)

Yes, Mrs. Evans.

NINA

(*Sternly.*)

For the sake of your future happiness and my son's I've got to speak! Your engagement forces me to! You've probably wondered why I objected. It's because the marriage is impossible. You can't marry Gordon! I speak as your friend! You must break your engagement with him at once!

MADELINE

(*Cannot believe her ears – suddenly panic-stricken.*)

But why – why?

DARRELL

(*Who has come closer – resentfully thinking.*)

She wants to ruin my son's life as she ruined mine! . . .

308

NINA

(Relentlessly.)

Why? Because —

DARRELL

(Steps up suddenly beside them – sharply and sternly commanding.)

No, Nina!

(He taps Madeline on the shoulder and draws her aside. Nina lets go of her wrist and stares after them in a sort of stunned stupor.)

Miss Arnold, as a doctor I feel it my duty to tell you that Mrs. Evans isn't herself. Pay no attention to anything she may say to you. She's just passed through a critical period in a woman's life and she's morbidly jealous of you and subject to queer delusions!

(He smiles kindly at her.)

So get back to the race! And God bless you!

(He grips her hand, strangely moved.)

MADELINE

(Gratefully.)

Thank you. I understand, I think. Poor Mrs. Evans!

(She hurries back to the rail, raising her glasses.)

NINA

(Springing to her feet and finding her voice – with despairing accusation.)

Ned!

309

DARRELL

(*Steps quickly to her side.*)

I'm sorry, Nina, but I warned you not to meddle.

(*Then affectionately.*)

And Gordon is – well – sort of my stepson, isn't he? I really want him to be happy.

(*Then smiling good-naturedly.*)

All the same, I can't help hoping he'll be beaten in this race. As an oarsman he recalls his father, Gordon Shaw, to me.

(*He turns away and raises his glasses, going back to the rail. Nina slumps down in her chair again.*)

EVANS

Damn! They all look even from here! Can you tell which is which, Madeline?

MADELINE

No – not yet – oh, dear, this is awful! Gordon!

NINA

(*Looking about her in the air – with a dazed question.*)

Gordon?

MARSDEN

(*Thinking.*)

Damn that Darrell! . . . if he hadn't interfered Nina would have told . . . something of infinite importance, I know! . . .

(*He comes and again sits on the deck by her chair and takes her hand.*)

Because what, Nina – my dear little Nina Cara Nina – because what? Let me help you!

NINA

(*Staring before her as if she were in a trance – simply, like a young girl.*)

Yes, Charlie. Yes, Father. Because all of Sam's father's family have been insane. His mother told me so that I wouldn't have his baby. I was going to tell Madeline so that she wouldn't marry Gordon. But it would have been a lie because Gordon isn't really Sam's child at all, he's Ned's. Ned gave him to me and I gave him to Sam so Sam could have a healthy child and be well and happy. And Sam is well and happy, don't you think?

(*Childishly.*)

So I haven't been such an awfully wicked girl, have I, Father?

MARSDEN

(*Horrified and completely sobered by what he has heard – stares at her with stunned eyes.*)

Nina! Good God! Do you know what you're saying?

MADELINE

(*Excitedly.*)

There! The one on this side! I saw the colour on their blades just now!

EVANS

(*Anxiously.*)

Are you sure? Then he's a little behind the other two!

DARRELL

(Excitedly.)

The one in the middle seems to be ahead! Is that the Navy?

> *(But the others pay no attention to him. All three are leaning over the rail, their glasses glued to their eyes, looking up the river. The noise from the whistle is now very loud. The cheering from the observation trains can be heard.)*

MARSDEN

(Stares into her face with great pity now.)

Merciful God, Nina! Then you've lived all these years – with this horror! And you and Darrell deliberately – ?

NINA

(Without looking at him – to the air.)

Sam's mother said I had a right to be happy, too.

MARSDEN

And you didn't love Darrell then – ?

NINA

(As before.)

I did afterwards. I don't now. Ned is dead, too.

(Softly.)

Only you are alive now, Father – and Gordon.

MARSDEN

(Gets up and bends over her paternally, stroking her hair with a strange, wild, joyous pity.)

Oh, Nina – poor little Nina – my Nina – how you must

have suffered! I forgive you! I forgive you everything! I forgive even your trying to tell Madeline – you wanted to keep Gordon – oh, I understand that – and I forgive you!

NINA

(*As before – affectionately and strangely.*)

And I forgive you, Father. It was all your fault in the beginning, wasn't it? You mustn't ever meddle with human lives again!

EVANS

(*Wildly excited.*)

Gordon's sprinting, isn't he? He's drawing up on that middle one!

MADELINE

Yes! Oh, come on, Gordon!

DARRELL

(*Exultantly.*)

Come on, Navy!

EVANS

(*Who is standing next to Ned, whirls on him in a furious passion.*)

What's that? What the hell's the matter with you?

DARRELL

(*Facing him – with a strange friendliness slaps him on the back.*)

We've got to beat these Gordons, Sam! We've got to beat –

313

EVANS

(*Raging.*)

You – !

> (*He draws back his fist – then suddenly horrified at what he is doing, but still angry, grabs Darrell by both shoulders and shakes him.*)

Wake up! What the hell's got into you? Have you gone crazy?

DARRELL

(*Mockingly.*)

Probably! It runs in my family! All of my father's people were happy lunatics – not healthy, country folk like yours, Sam! Ha!

EVANS

(*Staring at him.*)

Ned, old man, what's the trouble? You said "Navy."

DARRELL

(*Ironically – with a bitter hopeless laugh.*)

Slip of the tongue! I meant Gordon! Meant Gordon, of course! Gordon is always meant – meant to win! Come on, Gordon! It's fate!

MADELINE

Here they come! They're both spurting! I can see Gordon's back!

EVANS

(*Forgetting everything else, turns back to the race.*)

Come on, boy! Come on, son!

314

(The chorus of noise is now a bedlam as the crews near the finish line. The people have to yell and scream to make themselves heard.)

NINA

(Getting up – thinking with a strange, strident, wild passion.)

I hear the Father laughing! . . . O Mother God, protect my son! . . . let Gordon fly to you in heaven! . . . quick, Gordon! . . . love is the Father's lightning! . . . Madeline will bring you down in flames! . . . I hear His screaming laughter! . . . fly back to me! . . .

(She is looking desperately up into the sky as if some race of life and death were happening there for her.)

EVANS

(Holding on to a stanchion and leaning far out at the imminent risk of falling in.)

One spurt more will do it! Come on, boy, come on! It took death to beat Gordon Shaw! You can't be beaten either, Gordon! Lift her out of the water, son! Stroke! Stroke! He's gaining! Now! Over the line, boy! Over with her! Stroke! That's done it! He's won! He's won!

MADELINE

(Has been shrieking at the same time.)

Gordon! Gordon! He's won! Oh, he's fainted! Poor dear darling!

(She remains standing on the rail, looking out dangerously, holding on with one hand, looking down longingly toward his shell.)

EVANS

(Bounding back to the deck, his face congested and purple with a frenzy of joy, dancing about.)

He's won! By God, it was close! Greatest race in the history of rowing! He's the greatest oarsman God ever made!

(Embracing Nina and kissing her frantically.)

Aren't you happy, Nina? Our Gordon! The greatest ever!

NINA

(Torturedly – trying incoherently to force out a last despairing protest.)

No! – not yours! – mine! – and Gordon's! – Gordon is Gordon's! – he was my Gordon! – his Gordon is mine!

EVANS

(Soothingly, humouring her – kissing her again.)

Of course he's yours, dear – and a dead ringer for Gordon Shaw, too! Gordon's body! Gordon's spirit! Your body and spirit, too, Nina! He's not like me, lucky for him! I'm a poor boob! I never could row worth a damn!

(He suddenly staggers as if he were very drunk, leaning on Marsden – then gives a gasp and collapses inertly to the deck, lying on his back.)

MARSDEN

(Stares down at him stupidly – then thinking strangely.)

I knew it! . . . I saw the end beginning! . . .

(He touches Nina's arm – in a low voice.)

Nina – your husband!

(Touching Darrell who has stood staring straight before him, with a bitter ironical smile on his lips.)

Ned – your friend! Doctor Darrell – a patient!

NINA

(Stares down at Evans – slowly, as if trying to bring her mind back to him.)

My husband?

(Suddenly with a cry of pain, sinks on her knees beside the body.)

Sam!

DARRELL

(Looking down at him – thinking yearningly.)

Is her husband dead . . . at last? . . .

(Then with a shudder at his thoughts.)

No! . . . I don't hope! . . . I don't! . . .

(He cries:)

Sam!

(He kneels down, feels at his heart, pulse, looks into his face – with a change to a strictly professional manner.)

He's not dead. Only a bad stroke.

NINA

(With a cry of grief.)

Oh, Ned, did all our old secret hopes do this at last?

DARRELL

(Professionally, staring at her coldly.)

Bosh, Mrs. Evans! We're not in the Congo that we can believe in evil charms!

(Sternly.)

In his condition, Mr. Evans must have absolute quiet and

317

peace of mind or — And perfect care! You must tend him night and day! And I will! We've got to keep him happy!

NINA

(Dully.)

Again?

(Then sternly in her turn, as if swearing a pledge to herself.)

I will never leave his side! I will never tell him anything that might disturb his peace!

MARSDEN

(Standing above them — thinking exultantly.)
I shall not have long to wait now! . . .
(Then ashamed.)
How can I think such things . . . poor Sam! . . . he was . . . I mean he is my friend . . .
(With assertive loyalty.)

A rare spirit! A pure and simple soul! A good man — yes, a good man! God bless him!

(He makes a motion over the body like a priest blessing.)

DARRELL

(His voice suddenly breaking with a sincere human grief.)

Sam, old boy! I'm so damned sorry! I would give my life to save you!

NINA

(In dull anguish.)

Save — again?

(Then lovingly, kissing Evans' face.)

Dear husband, you have tried to make me happy, I will

318

give you my happiness again! I will give you Gordon to give
to Madeline!

MADELINE

(*Still standing on the rail, staring after Gordon's
shell.*)
Gordon! . . . dear lover . . . how tired . . . but you'll
rest in my arms . . . your head will lie on my breast . . .
soon! . . .

(Curtain.)

ACT NINE

SCENE: *Several months later. A terrace on the Evans' estate on Long Island. In the rear, the terrace overlooks a small harbour with the ocean beyond. On the right is a side entrance of the pretentious villa. On the left is a hedge with an arched gateway leading to a garden. The terrace is paved with rough stone. There is a stone bench at centre, a chaise longue at right, a wicker table and arm-chair at left.*

It is late afternoon of a day in early fall. Gordon Evans is sitting on the stone bench, his chin propped on his hands, Madeline standing behind him, her arm about his shoulders. Gordon is over six feet tall with the figure of a trained athlete. His sun-bronzed face is extremely handsome after the fashion of the magazine-cover American-collegian. It is a strong face but of a strength wholly material in quality. He has been too thoroughly trained to progress along a certain groove to success ever to question it or be dissatisfied with its rewards. At the same time, although entirely an unimaginative code-bound gentleman of his groove, he is boyish and likable, of an even, modest, sporting disposition. His expression is boyishly forlorn, but he is making a manly effort to conceal his grief.

Madeline is much the same as in the previous Act except that there is now a distinct maternal older feeling in her attitude toward Gordon as she endeavours to console him.

MADELINE

(*Tenderly, smoothing his hair.*)

There, dear! I know how horribly hard it is for you. I loved him, too. He was so wonderful and sweet to me.

GORDON

(*His voice trembling.*)

I didn't really realize he was gone – until out at the cemetery –

(*His voice breaks.*)

MADELINE

(*Kissing his hair.*)

Darling! Please don't!

GORDON

(*Rebelliously.*)

Damn it, I don't see why he had to die!

(*With a groan.*)

It was that constant grind at the office! I ought to have insisted on his taking better care of himself. But I wasn't home enough, that's the trouble. I couldn't watch him.

(*Then bitterly.*)

But I can't see why Mother didn't!

MADELINE

(*Reprovingly but showing she shares his feeling.*)

Now! You mustn't start feeling bitter toward her.

GORDON

(*Contritely.*)

I know I shouldn't.

(*But returning to his bitter tone.*)

But I can't help remembering how unreasonably she's acted about our engagement.

MADELINE

Not since your father was taken sick, she hasn't, dear.
She's been wonderfully nice.

GORDON

(*In the same tone.*)

Nice? Indifferent, you mean! She doesn't seem to care a
damn one way or the other any more!

MADELINE

You could hardly expect her to think of anyone but your
father. She's been with him every minute. I never saw such
devotion.

(*Thinking.*)

Will Gordon ever get old and sick like that? . . . oh, I
hope we'll both die before! . . . but I'd nurse him just as
she did his father . . . I'll always love him! . . .

GORDON

(*Consoled – proudly.*)

Yes, she sure was wonderful to him, all right!

(*Then coming back to his old tone.*)

But – this may sound rotten of me – I always had a queer
feeling she was doing it as a duty. And when he died, I felt
her grief was – not from love for him – at least, only the love
of a friend, not a wife's love.

(*As if under some urgent compulsion from within.*)

I've never told you, but I've always felt, ever since I was a
little kid, that she didn't really love Dad. She liked him and

respected him. She was a wonderful wife. But I'm sure she didn't love him.

(*Blurting it out as if he couldn't help it.*)

I'll tell you, Madeline! I've always felt she cared a lot for – Darrell.

(*Hastily.*)

Of course, I might be wrong.

(*Then bursting out.*)

No, I'm not wrong! I've felt it too strongly, ever since I was a kid. And then when I was eleven – something happened. I've been sure of it since then.

MADELINE

(*Thinking in amazement, but not without a queer satisfaction.*)

Does he mean that she was unfaithful to his father? . . . no, he'd never believe that . . . but what else could he mean? . . .

(*Wonderingly.*)

Gordon! Do you mean you've been sure that your mother was –

GORDON

(*Outraged by something in her tone – jumping to his feet and flinging her hand off – roughly.*)

Was what? What do you mean, Madeline?

MADELINE

(*Frightened – placatingly puts her arms around him.*)

I didn't mean anything, dear. I simply thought you meant –

323

GORDON

(*Still indignant.*)

All I mean was that she must have fallen in love with Darrell long after she was married – and then she sent him away for Dad's sake – and mine, too, I suppose. He kept coming back every couple of years. He didn't have guts enough to stay away for good! Oh, I suppose I'm unfair. I suppose it was damned hard on him. He fought it down, too, on account of his friendship for Dad.

(*Then with a bitter laugh.*)

I suppose they'll be getting married now! And I'll have to wish them good luck. Dad would want me to. He was game.

(*With a bitter gloomy air.*)

Life is damn queer, that's all I've got to say!

MADELINE

(*Thinking with a sort of tender, loving scorn for his boyish naïveté.*)

How little he knows her! . . . Mr. Evans was a fine man but . . . Darrell must have been fascinating once . . . if she loved anyone she isn't the kind who would hesitate . . . any more than I have with Gordon . . . oh, I'll never be unfaithful to Gordon . . . I'll love him always! . . .

(*She runs her fingers through his hair caressingly – comfortingly.*)

You must never blame them, dear. No one can help love. We couldn't, could we?

> '*She sits beside him. He takes her in his arms. They kiss each other with rising passion. Marsden comes in noiselessly from the garden, a bunch of roses and a pair of shears in his hands. He looks younger, calm and contented. He is dressed in*

*his all black, meticulous, perfectly tailored
mourning costume. He stands looking at the two
lovers, a queer agitation coming into his face.)*

MARSDEN

(Scandalized as an old maid – thinking.)
I must say! . . . his father hardly cold in his grave! . . .
it's positively bestial! . . .
*(Then struggling with himself – with a defensive
self-mockery.)*
Only it wasn't his father . . . what is Sam to Darrell's
son? . . . and even if he were Sam's son, what have the
living to do with the dead? . . . his duty is to love that life
may keep on living . . . and what has their loving to do
with me? . . . my life is cool green shade wherein comes no
scorching zenith sun of passion and possession to wither the
heart with bitter poisons . . . my life gathers roses, coolly
crimson, in sheltered gardens, on late afternoons in love
with evening . . . roses heavy with after-blooming of the
long day, desiring evening . . . my life is an evening . . .
Nina is a rose, my rose, exhausted by the long, hot day,
leaning wearily toward peace. . . .
*(He kisses one of the roses with a simple sentimental
smile – then still smiling, makes a gesture toward the two lovers.)*
That is on another planet, called the world . . . Nina and
I have moved on to the moon. . . .

MADELINE

(Passionately.)
Dear one! Sweetheart!

GORDON

Madeline! I love you!

325

MARSDEN

(*Looking at them – gaily mocking – thinking.*)
Once I'd have felt jealous . . . cheated . . . swindled by
God out of joy! . . . I would have thought bitterly, "The
Gordons have all the luck!" . . . but now I know that dear
old Charlie . . . yes, poor dear old Charlie! – passed beyond
desire, has all the luck at last! . . .

(*Then matter-of-factly.*)
But I'll have to interrupt their biological preparations . . .
there are many things still to be done this evening . . . Age's
terms of peace, after the long interlude of war with life, have
still to be concluded . . . Youth must keep decently away
. . . so many old wounds may have to be unbound, and old
scars pointed to with pride, to prove to ourselves we have
been brave and noble! . . .

(*He lets the shears drop to the ground. They jump
startledly and turn around. He smiles quietly.*)

Sorry to disturb you. I've been picking some roses for your
mother, Gordon. Flowers really have the power to soothe
grief. I suppose it was that discovery that led to their general
use at funerals – and weddings!

(*He hands a rose to Madeline.*)

Here, Madeline, here's a rose for you. Hail, Love, we who
have died, salute you!

(*He smiles strangely. She takes the rose automatically, staring at him uncomprehendingly.*)

MADELINE

(*Thinking suspiciously.*)
What a queer creature! . . . there's something uncanny!
. . . oh, don't be silly! . . . it's only poor old Charlie! . . .
(*She makes him a mocking curtsy.*)

Thank you, Uncle Charlie!

326

GORDON

(Thinking with sneering pity.)
Poor old guy! . . . he means well . . . Dad liked him. . . .
(Pretending an interest in the roses.)

They're pretty.

(Then suddenly.)

Where's Mother – still in the house?

MARSDEN

She was trying to get rid of the last of the people. I'm
going in. Shall I tell her you want to see her? It would give
her an excuse to get away.

GORDON

Yes. Will you?

(Marsden goes into the house on right.)

MADELINE

You'd better see your mother alone. I'll go down to the
'plane and wait for you. You want to fly back before dark,
don't you?

GORDON

Yes, and we ought to get started soon.

(Moodily.)

Maybe it would be better if you weren't here. There are
some things I feel I ought to say to her – and Darrell. I've
got to do what I know Dad would have wanted. I've got to
be fair. He always was to everyone all his life.

MADELINE

You dear, you! You couldn't be unfair to anyone if you tried!

> (*She kisses him.*)

Don't be too long.

GORDON

> (*Moodily.*)

You bet I won't! It won't be so pleasant I'll want to drag it out!

MADELINE

Good-bye for a while then.

GORDON

So long!

> (*He looks after her lovingly as she goes out right, rear, around the corner of the house.*)
> (*Thinking.*)

Madeline's wonderful! . . . I don't deserve my luck . . . but, God, I sure do love her! . . .

> (*He sits down on the bench again, his chin on his hands.*)

It seems rotten and selfish to be happy . . . when Dad . . . oh, he understands, he'd want me to be . . . it's funny how I got to care more for Dad than for Mother . . . I suppose it was finding out she loved Darrell . . . I can remember that day seeing her kiss him . . . it did something to me I never got over . . . but she made Dad happy . . . she gave up her own happiness for his sake . . . that was certainly damn fine . . . that was playing the game . . . I'm a hell of a one to criticize . . . my own mother! . . .

> (*Changing the subject of his thoughts abruptly.*)

Forget it! . . . think of Madeline . . . we'll be married

... then two months' honeymoon in Europe ... God, that'll be great! ... then back and dive into the business ... Dad relied on me to carry on where he left off ... I'll have to start at the bottom, but I'll get to the top in a hurry, I promise you that, Dad! ...

> (*Nina and Darrell come out of the house on the right. He hears the sound of the door and looks around.*)
> (*Thinking resentfully.*)

Funny! ... I can't stand it even now! ... when I see him with Mother! ... I'd like to beat him up! ...

> (*He gets to his feet, his face unconsciously becoming older and cold and severe. He stares accusingly at them as they come slowly toward him in silence. Nina looks much older than in the preceding Act. Resignation has come into her face, a resignation that uses no make-up, that has given up the struggle to be sexually attractive and look younger. She is dressed in deep black. Darrell's deep sunburn of the tropics has faded, leaving his skin a Mongolian yellow. He, too, looks much older. His expression is sad and bitter.*)

NINA

> (*Glancing at Gordon searchingly – thinking sadly.*)

He sent for me to say good-bye ... really good-bye for ever this time ... he's not my son now, nor Gordon's son, nor Sam's, nor Ned's ... he has become that stranger, another woman's lover. ...

DARRELL

> (*Also after a quick keen glance at Gordon's face – thinking.*)

There's something up ... some final accounting ...
> (*Thinking resignedly.*)

Well, let's get it over ... then I can go back to work,

. . . I've stayed too long up here . . . Preston must be wondering if I've deserted him. . . .

(*Then with a wondering sadness.*)

Is that my son? . . . my flesh and blood? . . staring at me with such cold enmity? . . . how sad and idiotic this all is! . . .

NINA

(*Putting on a tone of joking annoyance.*)

Your message was a godsend, Gordon. Those stupid people with their social condolences were killing me. Perhaps I'm morbid, but I always have the feeling that they're secretly glad someone is dead — that it flatters their vanity and makes them feel superior because they're living.

(*She sits wearily on the bench. Darrell sits on side of the* chaise longue *at right.*)

GORDON

(*Repelled by this idea — stiffly.*)

They were all good friends of Dad's. Why shouldn't they be sincerely sorry? His death ought to be a loss to everyone who knew him.

(*His voice trembles. He turns away and walks to the table.*)

(*Thinking bitterly.*)

She doesn't care a damn! . . . she's free to marry Darrell now! . . .

NINA

(*Thinking sadly, looking at his back.*)

He's accusing me because I'm not weeping . . . well, I did weep . . . all I could . . . there aren't many tears left . . . it was too bad Sam had to die . . . living suited him . . . he was so contented with himself . . . but I can't feel guilty

... I helped him to live ... I made him believe I loved
him ... his mind was perfectly sane to the end ... and
just before he died, he smiled at me ... so gratefully and
forgivingly, I thought ... closing our life together with
that smile ... that life is dead ... its regrets are dead
... I am sad, but there's comfort in the thought that now I
am free at last to rot away in peace ... I'll go and live in
Father's old home ... Sam bought that back ... I suppose he left it to me ... Charlie will come in every day to
visit ... he'll comfort and amuse me ... we can talk together of the old days ... when I was a girl ... when I
was happy ... before I fell in love with Gordon Shaw and
all this tangled mess of love and hate and pain and birth
began! ...

DARRELL

(Staring at Gordon's back resentfully.)
It gets under my skin to see him act so unfeelingly toward
his mother! ... if he only knew what she's suffered for his
sake! ... the Gordon Shaw ideal passed on through Sam
has certainly made my son an insensitive clod! ...
(With disgust.)
Bah, what has that young man to do with me? ...
compared to Preston he's only a well-muscled, handsome
fool! ...
(With a trace of anger.)
But I'd like to jolt his stupid self-complacency! ... if he
knew the facts about himself, he wouldn't be sobbing sentimentally about Sam ... he'd better change his tune or I'll
certainly be tempted to tell him ... there's no reason for
his not knowing now ...
*(His face is flushed. He has worked himself into a
real anger.)*

GORDON

*(Suddenly, having got back his control, turns to them
— coldly.)*

331

There are certain things connected with Dad's will I thought I ought to –

(With a tinge of satisfied superiority.)

I don't believe Dad told you about his will, did he, Mother?

NINA

(Indifferently.)

No.

GORDON

Well, the whole estate goes to you and me, of course. I didn't mean that.

(With a resentful look at Darrell.)

But there is one provision that is peculiar, to say the least. It concerns you, Doctor Darrell – a half-million for your Station to be used in biological research work.

DARRELL

(His face suddenly flushing with anger.)

What's that? That's a joke, isn't it?

(Thinking furiously.)

It's worse! . . . it's a deliberate insult! . . . a last sneer of ownership! . . . of my life! . . .

GORDON

(Coldly sneering.)

I thought it must be a joke myself – but Dad insisted.

DARRELL

(Angrily.)

Well, I won't accept it – and that's final!

GORDON

(*Coldly*.)

It's not left to you, but to the Station. Your supervision is mentioned, but I suppose if you won't carry on, whoever is in real charge down there will be only too glad to accept it.

DARRELL

(*Stupefied*.)

That means Preston! But Sam didn't even know Preston – except from hearing me talk about him! What had Sam to do with Preston? Preston is none of his business! I'll advise Preston to refuse it!

(*Thinking torturedly*.)

But it's for Science! . . . he has no right to refuse! . . . I have no right to ask him to! . . . God damn Sam! . . . wasn't it enough for him to own my wife, my son, in his lifetime? . . . now in death he reaches out to steal Preston! . . . to steal **my** work! . . .

NINA

(*Thinking bitterly*.)

Even in death Sam makes people suffer . . .

(*Sympathetically*.)

It isn't for you – nor for Preston. It's for Science, Ned. You must look at it that way.

GORDON

(*Thinking resentfully*.)

What a tender tone she takes toward him! . . . she's forgotten Dad already! . . .

(*With a sneer*.)

You'd better accept. Half-millions aren't being thrown away for nothing every day.

NINA

(*In anguish – thinking.*)
How can Gordon insult poor Ned like that! . . . his own father! . . . Ned has suffered too much! . . .
(*Sharply.*)

I think you've said about enough, Gordon!

GORDON

(*Bitterly, but trying to control himself – meaningly.*)

I haven't said all I'm going to say, Mother!

NINA

(*Thinking – at first frightenedly.*)
What does he mean? . . . does he know about Ned being . . . ?
(*Then with a sort of defiant relief.*)
Well, what does it matter what he thinks of me? . . . he's hers now, anyway. . . .

DARRELL

(*Thinking vindictively.*)
I hope he knows the truth, for if he doesn't, by God, I'll tell him! . . . if only to get something back from Sam of all he's stolen from me! . . .
(*Authoritatively – as Gordon hesitates.*)

Well, what have you got to say? Your mother and I are waiting.

GORDON

(*Furiously, taking a threatening step toward him.*)

Shut up, you! Don't take that tone with me or I'll forget your age –

(*Contemptuously.*)

and give you a spanking!

NINA

(*Thinking hysterically.*)
Spanking! . . . the son spanks the father! . . .
(*Laughing hysterically.*)

Oh, Gordon, don't make me laugh! It's all so funny!

DARRELL

(*Jumps from his chair and goes to her – solicitously.*)

Nina! Don't mind him! He doesn't realize –

GORDON

(*Maddened, comes closer.*)

I realize a lot! I realize you've acted like a cur!

(*He steps forward and slaps Darrell across the face viciously. Darrell staggers back from the force of the blow, his hands to his face. Nina screams and flings herself on Gordon, holding his arms.*)

NINA

(*Piteously – hysterically.*)

For God's sake, Gordon! What would your father say? You don't know what you're doing! You're hitting your father!

335

DARRELL

(*Suddenly breaking down – chokingly.*)

No – it's all right, son – all right – you didn't know –

GORDON

(*Crushed, overcome by remorse for his blow.*)

I'm sorry – sorry – you're right, Mother – Dad would feel as if I'd hit him – just as bad as if I'd hit him!

DARRELL

It's nothing, son – nothing!

GORDON

(*Brokenly.*)

That's damn fine, Darrell – damn fine and sporting of you! It was a rotten, dirty trick! Accept my apology, Darrell, won't you?

DARRELL

(*Staring at him stupidly – thinking.*)
Darrell? . . . he calls me Darrell! . . . but doesn't he know? . . . I thought she told him. . . .

NINA

(*Laughing hysterically – thinking.*)
I told him he hit his father . . . but he can't understand me! . . . why, of course he can't! . . . how could he? . .

GORDON

(*Insistently holding out his hand.*)

I'm damned sorry! I didn't mean it! Shake hands, won't you?

DARRELL

(*Doing so mechanically – stupidly.*)

Only too glad – pleased to meet you – know you by reputation – the famous oarsman – great race you stroked last June – but I was hoping the Navy would give you a beating.

NINA

(*Thinking in desperate hysterical anguish.*)

Oh, I wish Ned would go away and stay away for ever! . . . I can't bear to watch him suffer any more! . . . it's too frightful! . . . yes, God the Father, I hear you laughing . . . you see the joke . . . I'm laughing, too . . . it's all so crazy, isn't it? . . .

(*Laughing hysterically.*)

Oh, Ned! Poor Ned! You were born unlucky!

GORDON

(*Making her sit down again – soothing her.*)

Mother! Stop laughing! Please! It's all right – all right between us! I've apologized!

(*As she has grown calmer.*)

And now I want to say what I was going to say. It wasn't anything bad. It was just that I want you to know how fine I think you've both acted. I've known ever since I was a kid that you and Darrell were in love with each other. I hated the idea on Father's account – that's only natural, isn't it? – but I knew it was unfair, that people can't help loving each other any more than Madeline and I could have helped ourselves. And I saw how fair you both were to Dad – what a good wife you were, Mother – what a true friend you were, Darrell – and how damn much he loved you both! So all I

337

wanted to say is, now he's dead, I hope you'll get married and I hope you'll be as happy as you both deserve –

> (*Here he breaks down, kissing her and then breaking away.*)

I've got to say good-bye – got to fly back before dark – Madeline's waiting.

> (*He takes Darrell's hand and shakes it again. They have both been staring at him stupidly.*)

Good-bye, Darrell! Good luck!

DARRELL

> (*Thinking sufferingly.*)
> Why does he keep on calling me Darrell? . . . he's my boy. . . I'm his father . . . I've got to make him realize I'm his father! . . .
> (*Holding Gordon's hand.*)

Listen, son. It's my turn. I've got to tell you something –

NINA

> (*Thinking torturedly.*)
> Oh, he mustn't! . . . I feel he mustn't! . . .
> (*Sharply.*)

Ned! First, let me ask Gordon a question.

> (*Then looking her son in the eyes, slowly and impressively.*)

Do you think I was ever unfaithful to your father, Gordon?

GORDON

> (*Startled, stares at her – shocked and horrified – then suddenly he blurts out indignantly.*)

Mother, what do you think I am – as rotten-minded as that!

(*Pleadingly.*)

Please, Mother, I'm not as bad as that! I know you're the best woman that ever lived – the best of all! I don't even except Madeline!

NINA

(*With a sobbing triumphant cry.*)

My dear Gordon! You do love me, don't you?

GORDON

(*Kneeling beside her and kissing her.*)

Of course!

NINA

(*Pushing him away – tenderly.*)

And now go! Hurry! Madeline is waiting! Give her my love! Come to see me once in a while in the years to come! Good-bye, dear!

(*Turning to Darrell, who is standing with a sad resigned expression – imploringly.*)

Did you still want to tell Gordon something, Ned?

DARRELL

(*Forcing a tortured smile.*)

Not for anything in the world! Good-bye, son.

GORDON

Good-bye, sir.

(*He hurries off around the corner of the house at left, rear, thinking troubledly.*)

What does she think I am? . . . I've never thought that!

. . . I couldn't! . . . my own mother! I'd kill myself if I ever even caught myself thinking . . . !

(*He is gone.*)

NINA

(*Turns to Ned, gratefully taking his hand and pressing it.*)

Poor dear Ned, you've always had to give! How can I ever thank you?

DARRELL

(*With an ironical smile – forcing a joking tone.*)

By refusing me when I ask you to marry me! For I've got to ask you! Gordon expects it! And he'll be so pleased when he knows you turned me down.

(*Marsden comes out of the house.*)

Hallo, here comes Charlie! I must hurry. Will you marry me, Nina?

NINA

(*With a sad smile.*)

No. Certainly not. Our ghosts would torture us to death!

(*Then forlornly.*)

But I wish I did love you, Ned! Those were wonderful afternoons long ago! The Nina of those afternoons will always live in me, will always love her lover, Ned, the father of her baby!

DARRELL

(*Lifting her hand to his lips – tenderly.*)

Thank you for that! And that Ned will always adore his

340

beautiful Nina! Remember him! Forget me! I'm going
back to work.

(*He laughs softly and sadly.*)

I leave you to Charlie. You'd better marry him, Nina – if
you want peace. And after all, I think you owe it to him for
his lifelong devotion.

MARSDEN

(*Thinking uneasily.*)
They're talking about me . . . why doesn't he go? . . .
she doesn't love him any more . . . even now he's all heat
and energy and the tormenting drive of noon . . . can't he
see she is in love with evening? . . .
(*Clearing his throat uneasily.*)

Do I hear my name taken in vain?

NINA

(*Looking at Marsden with a strange yearning.*)
Peace! . . . yes . . . that is all I desire . . . I can no
longer imagine happiness . . . Charlie has found peace . . .
he will be tender . . . as my father was when I was a girl
. . . when I could imagine happiness . . .
(*With a girlish coquettishness and embarrassment –
making way for him on the bench beside her –
strangely.*)

Ned's just proposed to me. I refused him, Charlie. I don't
love him any more.

MARSDEN

(*Sitting down beside her.*)

I suspected as much. Then whom do you love, Nina Cara
Nina?

NINA

(*Sadly smiling.*)

You, Charlie, I suppose. I have always loved your love for me.

(*She kisses him – wistfully.*)

Will you let me rot away in peace?

MARSDEN

(*Strongly.*)

All my life I've waited to bring you peace.

NINA

(*Sadly teasing.*)

If you've waited that long, Charlie, we'd better get married to-morrow. But I forgot. You haven't asked me yet, have you? Do you want me to marry you, Charlie?

MARSDEN

(*Humbly.*)

Yes, Nina.

(*Thinking with a strange ecstasy.*)

I knew the time would come at last when I would hear her ask that! . . . I could never have said it, never! . . . oh, russet-golden afternoon, you are a mellow fruit of happiness ripely falling! . . .

DARRELL

(*Amused – with a sad smile.*)

Bless you, my children!

(*He turns to go.*)

342

NINA

I don't suppose we'll ever see you again, Ned.

DARRELL

I hope not, Nina. A scientist shouldn't believe in ghosts.
(*With a mocking smile.*)
But perhaps we'll become part of cosmic positive and negative electric charges and meet again.

NINA

In our afternoons – again?

DARRELL

(*Smiling sadly.*)
Again. In our afternoons.

MARSDEN

(*Coming out of his day dream.*)
We'll be married in the afternoon, decidedly. I've already picked out the church, Nina – a grey ivied chapel, full of restful shadow, symbolical of the peace we have found. The crimsons and purples in the windows will stain our faces with faded passion. It must be in the hour before sunset when the earth dreams in afterthoughts and mystic premonitions of life's beauty. And then we'll go up to your old home to live. Mine wouldn't be suitable for us. Mother and Jane live there in memory. And I'll work in your father's old study. He won't mind me.

STRANGE INTERLUDE

(*From the bay below comes the roaring hum of an aeroplane motor. Nina and Darrell jump startledly and go to the rear of the terrace to watch the 'plane ascend from the water, standing side by side. Marsden remains oblivious.*)

NINA

(*With anguish.*)

Gordon! Good-bye, dear!

(*Pointing as the 'plane climbs higher, moving away off to the left – bitterly.*)

See, Ned! He's leaving me without a backward look!

DARRELL

(*Joyfully.*)

No! He's circling. He's coming back!

(*The roar of the engine grows steadily nearer now.*)

He's going to pass directly over us!

(*Their eyes follow the 'plane as it comes swiftly nearer and passes directly over them.*)

See! He's waving to us!

NINA

Oh, Gordon! My dear son!

(*She waves frantically.*)

DARRELL

(*With a last tortured protest.*)

Nina! Are you forgetting? He's my son, too!

(*He shouts up at the sky.*)

344

You're my son, Gordon! You're my –

> (*He controls himself abruptly – with a smile of cynical self-pity.*)

He can't hear! Well, at least I've done my duty!

> (*Then with a grim fatalism – with a final wave of his hand at the sky.*)

Good-bye, Gordon's son!

NINA

(*With tortured exultance.*)

Fly up to heaven, Gordon! Fly with your love to heaven! Fly always! Never crash to earth like my old Gordon! Be happy, dear! You've got to be happy!

DARRELL

(*Sardonically.*)

I've heard that cry for happiness before, Nina! I remember hearing myself cry it – once – it must have been long ago! I'll get back to my cells – sensible unicellular life that floats in the sea and has never learned the cry for happiness! I'm going, Nina.

> (*As she remains oblivious, staring after the 'plane – thinking fatalistically.*)
> She doesn't hear, either. . . .
> (*He laughs up at the sky.*)
> Oh, God, so deaf and dumb and blind! . . . teach me to be resigned to be an atom! . . .
> (*He walks off, right, and enters the house.*)

NINA

(*Finally lowering her eyes – confusedly.*)

Gone! My eyes are growing dim. Where is Ned? Gone,

too. And Sam is gone. They're all dead. Where are Father and Charlie?

> (*With a shiver of fear she hurries over and sits on the bench beside Marsden, huddling against him.*)

Gordon is dead, Father. I've just had a cable. What I mean is, he flew away to another life – my son, Gordon, Charlie. So we're alone again – just as we used to be.

MARSDEN

> (*Putting his arm around her – affectionately.*)

Just as we used to be, dear Nina Cara Nina, before Gordon came.

NINA

> (*Looking up at the sky – strangely.*)

My having a son was a failure, wasn't it? He couldn't give me happiness. Sons are always their fathers. They pass through the mother to become their father again. The Sons of the Father have all been failures! Failing they died for us, they flew away to other lives, they could not stay with us, they could not give us happiness!

MARSDEN

> (*Paternally – in her father's tone.*)

You had best forget the whole affair of your association with the Gordons. After all, dear Nina, there was something unreal in all that has happened since you first met Gordon Shaw, something extravagant and fantastic, the sort of thing that isn't done, really, in our afternoons. So let you and me forget the whole distressing episode, regard it as an interlude, of trial and preparation, say, in which our souls have been scraped clean of impure flesh and made worthy to bleach in peace.

NINA

(*With a strange smile.*)

Strange interlude! Yes, our lives are merely strange dark interludes in the electrical display of God the Father!

(*Resting her head on his shoulder.*)

You're so restful, Charlie. I feel as if I were a girl again and you were my father and the Charlie of those days made into one. I wonder is our old garden the same? We'll pick flowers together in the ageing afternoons of spring and summer, won't we? It will be a comfort to get home – to be old and to be home again at last – to be in love with peace together – to love each other's peace – to sleep with peace together –!

(*She kisses him – then shuts her eyes with a deep sigh of requited weariness.*)

– to die in peace! I'm so contentedly weary with life!

MARSDEN

(*With a serene peace.*)

Rest, dear Nina.

(*Then tenderly.*)

It has been a long day. Why don't you sleep now – as you used to, remember? – for a little while?

NINA

(*Murmurs with drowsy gratitude.*)

Thank you, Father – have I been wicked? – you're so good – dear old Charlie!

MARSDEN

> (*Reacting automatically and wincing with pain—thinking mechanically.*)

God damn dear old . . . !

> (*Then with a glance down at Nina's face, with a happy smile.*)

No, God bless dear old Charlie . . . who, passed beyond desire, has all the luck at last! . . .

> (*Nina has fallen asleep. He watches with contented eyes the evening shadows closing in around them.*)

(Curtain.)